NELSON

S
-
D

SUSAN SHEERIN

Si *ture*

inners

Thomas Nelson and Sons Ltd
Nelson House
Mayfield Road
Walton-on-Thames Surrey
KT12 5PL UK

51 York Place
Edinburgh
EH1 3JD UK

Thomas Nelson (Hong Kong) Ltd
Toppan Building 10/F
22A Westlands Road
Quarry Bay Hong Kong

First published by Thomas Nelson and Sons Ltd 1993

ISBN 0-17-556 - 399 - 3
NPN 9 8 7 6 5 4 3 2

Printed in Hong Kong

Produced by AMR

Acknowledgements

The authors and publishers would also like to thank the following for
permission to use photographs:

Biofotos 73(×8); Stuart Boreham 7, 15, 88, 116(×2); Busch Gardens,
Tampa 65; Colorsport 47(×6); Greg Evans 31(×2), 39, 77, 78(×4), 84,
104, 105; Ffotograff 92; Huchison Library 93; Image Bank 106;
Kishimoto Corporation 78; Network South East 15; Picturepoint 78;
Rex Features 66, 78, 105, 122(×2), 123(×5); Chris Ridgers 7(×4), 15(×4),
18, 20, 25, 41(×6), 42, 48, 52, 78, 93, 110, 126, 127(×3), 128, 130;
Angus Ross 59(×4); Still-moving Picture Company 27(×4); Telegraph
Colour Library 79; Tony Stone Worldwide 12, 15, 36, 58, 60, 64, 65, 77,
82; Zefa Picture Library 6, 8, 24, 30, 48, 58, 64, 65(×2), 66(×2), 82(×2), 106.

Illustrations by Susan Andre, Louise Banks, Josephine Blake,
Janice Bocquillon, Olivia Bown, Derek Brazell, Phillip Burrows,
Jane Cheswright, Jon Davis, Jo Dennis, John Fraser, Alice Garside,
Veronica Jones, Fiona Keen, Nina O'Connell, Stan Stevens.

Recording

The authors would like to thank Jenny Hardacre and Andrea Fischer for
their help with recordings.

CONTENTS

CONTENTS CHART

	Unit	Structures	Vocabulary	Functions	Pronunciation	Study Skills
PLACES	10	present continuous for future *want* + *to* + verb *go* + *-ing* (one-syllable) adjectives: comparative	weather holidays animals travel plans	telling the time opinions making plans	contractions	spelling rules information transfer (reading) writing a postcard
	11	present continuous for temporary situations possessive pronouns *whose*, *which* in questions	wildlife animals a conference	agreeing disagreeing ordering food saying goodbye	sentence rhythm and stress	analysing language
	12	simple past (irregular) verbs with two objects functions of adverbs *vs* adjectives	countries nationalities games, races study subjects	asking for and giving personal information describing flags	word stress on nouns vs adjectives	spelling rules

Revision Unit 2

	Unit	Structures	Vocabulary	Functions	Pronunciation	Study Skills
CHANGES	13	simple past (regular) more simple past verbs (irregular) and multi-word verbs	school subjects buildings appearance feelings	describing people	*-ed* in past tense (regular) verbs word stress: words ending in *-y*	spelling rules writing a short story
	14	*going to* + verb verbs with *back* verbs with two objects	love marriage objects materials	possession asking for and giving reasons future plans	/iː/ vs /ɪ/	word-building: *-un* using a spidergram
	15	*have to* including negative, vs *must* *going to* for future based on present evidence	renting a flat housework a party	conversation: changing topic of conversation	*have to* *has to* (weak forms)	phonetic script and pronunciation
	16	adjectives: comparatives and superlatives two-syllable adjectives ending in *-y*; irregulars	migration nationalities geography materials	comparing giving opinions	word stress dates	language learning strategies
	17	*used to* two- and three- syllable adjectives: comparatives and superlatives	competitions occupations lifestyles	asking for and giving opinions talking about the past	*used to* (weak forms)	making sentences from substitution tables writing an essay
	18	Pronouns: *one(s)* *so* and *neither* for agreeing and disagreeing	a job interview work the office machines	at an interview making an appointment agreeing disagreeing	weak forms contractions and sentence stress	

Revision Unit 3

UNIT 1 CAMPING HOLIDAY IN BRITAIN

A New friends

1 📻 Reading and Listening

Read and listen.

This is Michel. He's a teacher from France.
And this is his wife Marie. She is a teacher too.

a

Michel and Marie are on holiday in Britain.

John: 'Morning!
Michel: Good morning!
John: Can I help?

c

Michel: Thank you! ... Thanks!
John: Oh, it's OK.

d

Michel: My name's Michel. I'm from Brittany, in France.
John: Hello, Michel. I'm John. John Lott ...

e

John: ... and this is my wife, Helen.
We're from Bristol.

f

Michel: Ah ... this is *my* wife. Marie, this is John and this is Helen. They're from Bristol.
Marie: Hello, John. Hello, Helen.
John and Helen: Hello, Marie.

2 📻 Pronunciation

A Listen and repeat.

1 /θ/ = 'th' – thank you, thanks, three
2 /ð/ = 'th' – this, they're, they, the

B Listen and repeat.

1 Can I ... /kən aɪ/
2 Can I help? /kən aɪ help/

C Practise with a partner:

1 'This is Marie.'   2 'Can I help?'
'Hello!'   '_____ you!'
'And this is John.'   'Oh, it's OK.'

3 Speaking and Language Practice (C1.1, 1.3, 3.1)

New friends and introductions.

1

Hello. My name's Liisa. I'm from Helsinki.

Hello. I'm Jens. I'm from Zurich.

Now practise with a partner. Say *your* name and say where you are from.

2

Hello. I'm Liisa, and this is Jens. I'm from Helsinki, and he's from Zurich.

Hello. I'm Violetta. I'm from Stockholm.

or

Hi. I'm Liisa, and this is Merja. We're from Finland – I'm from Helsinki and she's from Tampere.

Hi. I'm Violetta. I'm from Stockholm.

Now practise in groups of three. Say your name and introduce your friend.

3

Hi. I'm Liisa, and this is Merja. We're from Finland. And this is Daniele. He's from Milan.

Hello. I'm Naoko. I'm from Tokyo.

Now practise in groups of four. Say your name and introduce your friends.

4 🔊 Study Skills

A Spelling (C4.1)

1 Listen and repeat.

A, B, C, D, E, F, G, H, I, J, K, L, M, N, O, P, Q, R, S, T, U, V, W, X, Y, Z

2 Spell!

Example: 'Capital F – r – a – n – c – e'

a France	**g** Paris
b Oxford	**h** Volkswagen
c John	**i** Yevtushenko
d Helen	**j** Michel
e Britain	**k** Quebec
f Zurich	**l** Marie

3 Listen and repeat.

'What's your name?'
'Adams ... John Adams.'
'Can you spell 'Adams'?'
'*Capital A – d – a – m – s.*'
'Thank you.'

Now you. Practise with a partner. Spell *your* name.

B Numbers (C4.2)

1 Listen and repeat.

1 one	2 two	3 three	4 four
5 five	6 six	7 seven	8 eight
9 nine	10 ten	11 eleven	
12 twelve			

2 Say the numbers. Practise with a partner.

B The Lebrun family and the Lott family

1 📼 *Listening and Writing*

Michel is on holiday at Oakland Camping. Mary is from Oakland Camping. She asks
Michel questions. You are Mary. Listen and write the answers.

❀❀❀ OAKLAND CAMPING ❀❀❀

You

Mr/Mrs/Miss/Ms

Surname: _____   First name: _____
Nationality: _____   Passport number: _____
Occupation: _____   Car number: _____
Address: _____

_____ BRITTANY _____

Wife/Husband

Surname: _____   First name: _____
Nationality: _____ CANADIAN _____   Occupation: _____

Children

1 Name: _____ Age: _____   2 Name: _____ Age: _____
3 Name: _____ Age: _____   4 Name: _____ Age: _____

Signature: Michel Lebrun

2 📼 *Vocabulary and Listening (C1.5 and 2.1)*

A Listen and write the names.

Henry Pamela Edith Kathleen Paul Tony Helen Sam Emily

1 _____ ┬ 2 _____   3 _____ ┬ 4 _____

5 _____   John Lott ─┬ 6 _____   7 _____

8 _____   9 _____

B Write the words in the sentences on page 9.

David ─┬ Fabienne   Anton ─┬ Elsa

Michel ─┬ Marie   Eva   Carl

Josephe   Patricia

1 David and Fabienne have one c..........d, Michel.
2 Michel is Marie's h.......... .
3 Marie is Michel's w.......... .
4 Michel and Marie have a s.......... , Josephe, and a d.......... , Patricia.
5 Patricia and Josephe are Marie's c.......... .
6 Josephe is Patricia's b.......... and Patricia is Josephe's s.......... .
7 Josephe and Patricia have an a.......... , Eva, and an u.......... , Carl.
8 Michel and Marie are Josephe's p.......... .
9 Anton and Elsa are Patricia's g.......... .
10 Anton is Marie's f......... and Elsa is her m.......... .
11 Anton is Josephe's g.......... .
12 And Elsa is Josephe's g.......... .

3 Language Practice (C1.1, 1.2, 1.7)

A Write: *my your his her our their.*

1 I'm John and this is .... wife, Helen.
2 This is .... son, Sam .
3 ... and .... sister, Emily.
4 Emily is seven and .... brother's eight.
5 Is this .... friend, Sam?
6 This is Josephe and Patricia. They and .... parents are from France.

B Write: *is 's isn't 'm 're are aren't.*

Example: **1** *This is my friend, Charles.*

1 This / my friend, Michel.
2 These / his children, Patricia and Josephe.
3 My name / John.
4 We / from Bristol.
5 Patricia and Josephe / from France.
6 Hello. I / Sam.
7 Josephe / from Normandy.
8 John and Helen / from Oxford.

4 Listening

Listen and match the pictures.

Example: *number **1** – picture **d**.*

a

b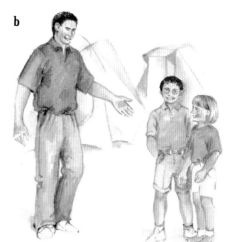

c

d

e

f

5 Speaking

Practise with a partner. Student A look at page 125. Student B answer your partner's questions.

C Language Study

1 GRAMMAR

1.1 The verb *to be*

I	'm	Michel.	(I	am	Michel.)
You	're	John.	(You	are	John.)
He	's	eight.	(He	is	eight.)
She	's	five.	(She	is	five.)
It	's	OK.	(It	is	OK.)
We	're	from France.	(We	are	from France.)
They	're	from Oxford.	(They	are	from Oxford.)

1.2 The negative of *to be*

I	'm not	Helen...I'm Marie.	(I	am not	Helen.)
You	aren't	John...you're Sam.	(You	are not	John.)
He	isn't	eight...he's ten.	(He	is not	eight.)
She	isn't	five...she's four.	(She	is not	five.)
It	isn't	OK.	(It	is not	OK.)
We	aren't	from France.	(We	are not	from France.)
They	aren't	from Oxford.	(They	are not	from Oxford.)

1.3 Pronouns

I

you

he

she

it

we

you

they

1.4 Nouns: Singular and Plural

Singular	Plural
a picture	two picture**s**

Irregular:

a child	two child**ren**

1.5 Nouns -'s

Michel**'s** wife (NOT: ~~The wife of Michel~~)

Josephe and Patricia**'s** grandfather
(NOT: ~~The grandfather of Patricia and Josephe~~)

1.6 The Indefinite Article: *a* and *an*

a [p] icture **a** [v] isitor

a, e, i, o, u:

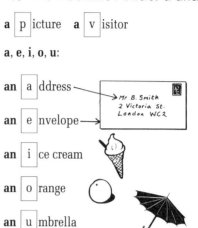

an [a] ddress

an [e] nvelope

an [i] ce cream

an [o] range

an [u] mbrella

1.7 Possessive Adjectives

I	→	**my**	we	→ **our**
you	→	**your**	they	→ **their**
he	→	**his**		
she	→	**her**		
it	→	**its**		

1.8 Prepositions

Landerneau's **in** Brittany.

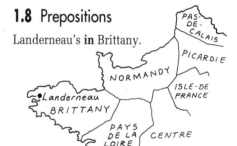

It's **from** France.

with a partner

2 VOCABULARY

2.1 A family

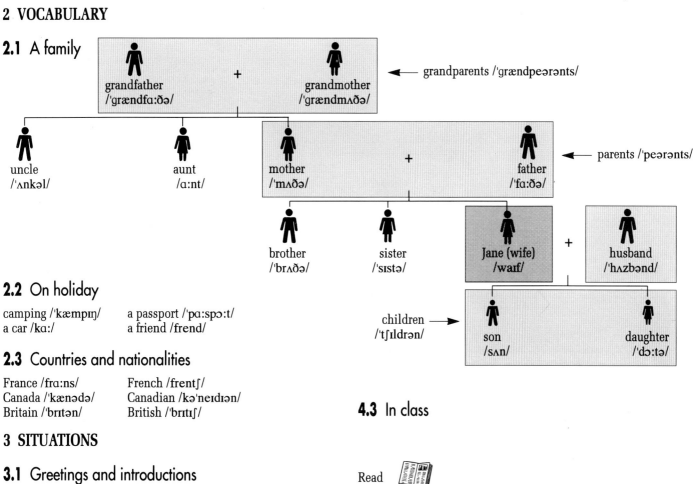

grandfather /'grændfɑːðə/

grandmother /'grændmʌðə/

grandparents /'grændpeərənts/

uncle /'ʌnkəl/

aunt /ɑːnt/

mother /'mʌðə/

father /'fɑːðə/

parents /'peərənts/

brother /'brʌðə/

sister /'sɪstə/

Jane (wife) /waɪf/

husband /'hʌzbənd/

children /'tʃɪldrən/

son /sʌn/

daughter /'dɔːtə/

2.2 On holiday

camping /'kæmpɪŋ/   a passport /'pɑːspɔːt/
a car /kɑː/   a friend /frend/

2.3 Countries and nationalities

France /frɑːns/   French /frentʃ/
Canada /'kænədə/   Canadian /kə'neɪdɪən/
Britain /'brɪtən/   British /'brɪtɪʃ/

3 SITUATIONS

3.1 Greetings and introductions

'Hello/Hi!'   'Good morning/Morning!'

'I'm Michel. I'm from Brittany.'

'This is Keiko. She's from Tokyo.'
'This is Pedro. He's from Madrid.'

3.2 Friends and family

'Thank you/Thanks!'
'Can I help?'
'Have a good holiday!'

4 LEARNING ENGLISH

4.1 Letters

Aa /eɪ/ Bb /biː/ Cc /siː/ Dd /diː/ Ee /iː/ Ff /ef/ Gg /dʒiː/
Hh /eɪtʃ/ Ii /aɪ/ Jj /dʒeɪ/ Kk /keɪ/ Ll /el/ Mm /em/
Nn /en/ Oo /əʊ/ Pp /piː/ Qq /kjuː/ Rr /ɑː/ Ss /es/
Tt /tiː/ Uu /juː/ Vv /viː/ Ww ('double u') /dʌbl juː/
Xx /eks/ Yy /waɪ/ Zz /zed/

4.2 Numbers

1 one /wʌn/   5 five /faɪv/   9 nine /naɪn/
2 two /tuː/   6 six /sɪks/   10 ten /ten/
3 three /θriː/   7 seven /sevən/   11 eleven /ɪ'levən/
4 four /fɔː/   8 eight /eɪt/   12 twelve /twelv/

4.3 In class

Read

Write (the words)

Listen

Speak (about the pictures)

Match

Practise (in groups of three)

Now you

UNIT 2 TONY DAY FROM AUSTRALIA

A In Customs

1 ▣Listening and Writing (C1.1 and 1.2)

A Listen and read.

Tony:	Can I help you?
Tourist:	Oh, thank you.
Tony:	It's OK.

Tony:	Are you on holiday?
Tourist:	Yes.
Tony:	Where are you from?
Tourist:	From France. And you?
Tony:	From Australia.

Customs Officer:	Is this your bag?
Tony:	Sorry?
Customs Officer:	Is this your bag?
Tony:	Yes, it is.
Customs Officer:	What's this?
Tony:	It's my camera. I'm a photographer.
Customs Officer:	And what are these?
Tony:	They're films.
Customs Officer:	OK. Thank you.

Now you. Practise with a partner.

B Now write
six sentences about you
and your friend.
Use *am/am not, is/isn't, are/aren't*.

1 I .... / ....
2 My friend .... / ....
3 We .... / ....

2 ▣Language Practice (C1.1 and 1.2)

Listen and read.

a

'Is this the bus for London?'
'No, it isn't. It's over there.'
'Thanks.'

b

'Is this the bus for London?'
'Yes, it is.'
'Thanks.'

c

'Sorry.'
'It's OK.'

3 🔊 *Pronunciation (C3.1 and 3.2)*

Listen. *Sorry?* or *Sorry.*

4   Reading and Writing (C2.2 and 2.3)

Work with a partner. Match the words with the pictures.

SNACK BAR	UNDERGROUND
MEETING POINT	TAXIS
INFORMATION	RESTAURANT
CHECK-IN DESK	CUSTOMS
PASSPORT CONTROL	TOILETS

B At the airport

1 ▭Language Practice and Listening (C1.3 and 1.4)

Listen and write.

1 'Excuse me. Where's the .... ?'
'It's over there.'

'And where's the .... ?'
'It's here.'

2 'Excuse me. Where are the .... ?'
'They're over there.

'And where are the .... ?'
'They're here.'

2 Speaking (C1.4)

Practise with a partner. Student A turn to page 125. Student B turn to page 127.

3 ▭Language Practice and Listening (C2.5 and 3.4)

Listen and write.

1 'How much is .... , please?'
'It's £ ....'

2 'How much is .... , please?'
'It's £ ....'

3 'How much are .... , please?'
'They're .... pence.'

4 'How much are .... , please?'
'They're .... pence.'

5 'How much .... this, please?'
'It's £ ....'

6 'How much .... that, please?'
'It's £ ....'

7 'How much .... these, please?'
'They're £ ....'

8 'How much .... those, please?'
'They're £ ....'

Now you. Practise with a partner.

4 Vocabulary and Study Skills

Practise with a partner:

'Excuse me, what's this/that in English?'
'It's a car.'

5 Spelling and Pronunciation (C1.5)

What are the plurals of the words in Exercise 4?
Say the words.

6 Listening and Pronunciation (C3.1 and 3.2)

Listen and match the numbers with the letters.

Example: **1 – d**

1 – **d**   2 – ......   3 – ......   4 – ......   5 – ......   6 – ......

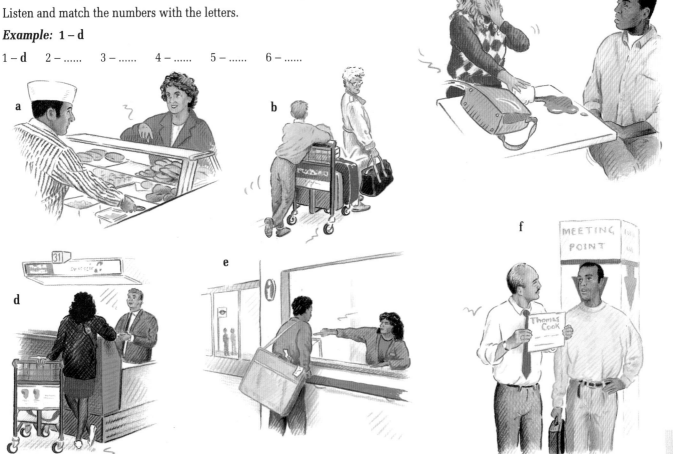

C Language Study

1 GRAMMAR

1.1 *to be:* Questions

1	2	3
Am	I	at the airport?
Are	you	Tony?
Is	she	your daughter?
Is	John	your husband?
Is	this	your friend?
Are	we	in Britain?
Are	they	Tony's bags?

1.2 *to be:* Short answers

'Is that the bus for London?' **'Yes, it is.'**
'Are these your passports?' **'Yes, they are.'**

'Is this your camera?' **'No, it isn't.'**
'Are these your bags?' **'No, they aren't.'**

1.3 Wh- questions + *to be*

1	2	3
Where	is	the restaurant?
	are	the buses?
	are	you from?
What	is	that?
	are	those?
How much	is	the cake?
	are	the watches?

1.4 Adverbs of Place

Here's the bus for the airport.
Here are our friends.
The car's **here**.
The toilets are **here**.

There's the bar.
There are John and Helen.

The shop's **over there**.
The taxis are **over there**.

1.5 Nouns: Singular and Plural

Singular	Plural
a bus	two buses /'bʌsɪz/
a watch	two watches /'wɒtʃɪz/

1.6 Demonstrative Pronouns: *this/that/these/those*

Examples: *How much is **this**?*

***That** is my bag.*

*How much are **these**?*

***Those** are my books.*

1.7 The Definite Article: *the*

'Is this **the** bus for London?' 'Where are **the** toilets?'

1.8 Prepositions

at (the airport)	**on** (the plane)
for (London)	**in** (the car)
under (the picture)	**in** (Customs)

2 VOCABULARY

2.1 Tony and his things

a photographer /fə'tɒgrəfə/
from Australia /frəm ɒ'streɪlɪə/
an Australian /ɒ'streɪlɪən/
a bag /bæg/
a film /fɪlm/
a camera /'kæmrə/
a passport /'pɑ:spɔ:t/

2.2 Transport

a bus /bʌs/
a taxi /'tæksɪ/
a plane /pleɪn/
a train /treɪn/
the underground /ðɪ 'ʌndəgraʊnd/

2.3 At the airport

a restaurant /'restrɒnt/
a shop /ʃɒp/
a snack bar /snæk bɑ:/
a bank /bæŋk/
a toilet /'tɔɪlət/
a cake /keɪk/
a watch /wɒtʃ/
a tourist /'tʊərɪst/

2.4 Numbers

13 thirteen /θɜ:'ti:n/
14 fourteen /fɔ:'ti:n/
15 fifteen /fɪf'ti:n/
16 sixteen /sɪks'ti:n/
17 seventeen /sevən'ti:n/
18 eighteen /eɪ'ti:n/
19 nineteen /naɪn'ti:n/

20 twenty /'twentɪ/
21 twenty one /'twentɪ wʌn/
22 twenty two /'twentɪ tu:/
23 twenty three /'twentɪ θri:/
24 twenty four /'twentɪ fɔ:/
25 twenty five /'twentɪ faɪv/
26 twenty six /'twentɪ sɪks/
27 twenty seven /'twentɪ sevən/
28 twenty eight /'twentɪ eɪt/
29 twenty nine /'twentɪ naɪn/

30 thirty /'θɜ:tɪ/
40 forty /'fɔ:tɪ/
50 fifty /'fɪftɪ/
60 sixty /'sɪkstɪ/
70 seventy /'sevəntɪ/
80 eighty /'eɪtɪ/
90 ninety /'naɪntɪ/
100 a hundred /ə 'hʌndrəd/

2.5 Money

£20 twenty pounds /'twentɪ paʊndz/
40p forty pence /'fɔ:tɪ pens/
£2.50 two pound(s) fifty /tu: paʊndz 'fɪftɪ/

3 SITUATIONS

3.1 Conversation

'Where are you from?'

'Are you on holiday?'

'Excuse me.'

'Sorry?'

3.2 Apologising

'Sorry.'

3.3 Asking for information

'Excuse me. Is this the bus for London?'

'Where is the restaurant?'

3.4 In a shop

'Can I help you?'
'How much is this, please?'
'How much are those, please?'
'Two cakes, please.'

4 LEARNING ENGLISH

'Sorry?'

'What's this in English?'
'What's that in English?'

'Turn to page 5.'

UNIT 3 ELISABETH SCHAEFFER FROM GERMANY

A At home and at college

1 ▣ Listening and Reading

Elisabeth Schaeffer is from Germany. She's on an English course in Oxford, and she has a room with Mr and Mrs White.

A Listen and read.

a

Mrs White: This is my husband, Tom. Tom, this is Elisabeth.
Elisabeth: How do you do, Mr White.
Mr White: How do you do, Elisabeth. Welcome to Oxford.
Elisabeth: Thank you.

b

Mrs White: This is the living room. Ah... and here are the children. Jane ... Richard, say hello to Elisabeth.
The children: Hi, Elisabeth!
Elisabeth: Hello.
Mrs White: They watch television a lot!

c

Mrs White: This is the kitchen. We have breakfast in here ... at about eight. Is that OK for you?
Elisabeth: Oh yes, that's fine.

d

Mrs White: This is the dining room. We have dinner in here at about seven o'clock.
Elisabeth: It's a nice room and the garden's lovely, too ...

e

Mrs White: This is Tom's study. He's an accountant and he works at home.
Elisabeth: I see.

f

Elisabeth: Is this Jane's bedroom?
Mrs White: Yes, that's right!

g

Mrs White: Here is the bathroom. You can have a shower or a bath any time.
Elisabeth: OK, thank you.

h

Mrs White: And this is your room.
Elisabeth: Oh, it's lovely! Thank you. I like it very much.

B Write the words in the sentences.

has	like	watch	have	works

1 They .... television.
2 We .... breakfast at about eight o'clock.
3 I .... it very much.
4 He .... at home.
5 She .... a shower at about seven o'clock.

2 Language Practice (C3.3)

A Telling the time: *What's the time?*
              It's **one o'clock**.

Now you. Practise with a partner. Ask the time and answer.

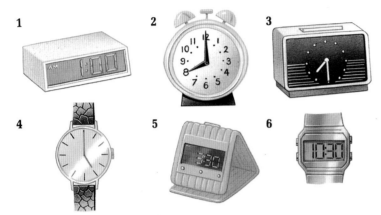

B

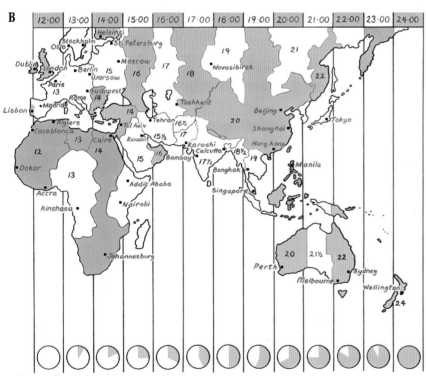

In London the time is ten o'clock in the morning. Practise with a partner.
Ask: *What's the time in* .... *?* and answer.

Example: *What's the time in* **Paris**?
                It's **eleven o'clock**

3 Language Practice (C1.1, 2.1)

Write the sentences.

Example: **1** *Elisabeth likes her room.*

1 Elisabeth / like / her room.
2 She / go / college
3 Elisabeth / English class / Wednesday afternoon.
4 Mr and Mrs White / breakfast /
5 The children / television / evening.
6 Elisabeth / shower / morning.
7 Elisabeth / get up /
8 Mr White / work / home.

4 Speaking (C3.1)

New friends: **A:** How do you do, ...
                       B: How do you do.
                              Welcome to .... .

Paris	Rome	Berlin	Pisa
London	Copenhagen		

Now you. Practise with a partner.

5 Vocabulary (C2.7)

Here is a plan of Mr and Mrs White's house.

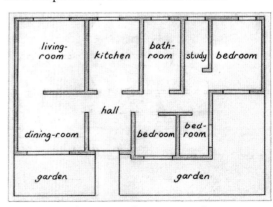

Now draw a plan of your home. Write the names of the rooms on the plan.

B Elisabeth's day

1 🎧 Listening (C1.1 and 1.2)

A Elisabeth meets a new student, Ricardo, at college.
Listen and answer the questions.

1 Where is Elisabeth from?
2 Where is Ricardo from?
3 Where is Elena from?

B Elisabeth and Ricardo talk about the college.
Listen and write the words Elisabeth says.

1 I .... the lessons very much.
2 We .... a lot.
3 We .... books and newspapers.
4 We .... cassettes.
5 Yes, sometimes. It's difficult but it's useful, I ....
6 I .... in the library for about an hour.
7 Then I .... home.
8 I .... dinner with Mr and Mrs White.
9 I .... my homework.
10 I .... television or go out with my friends.

C Listen again and match the answers in Exercise 1B to Ricardo's questions.

1 Do you learn English grammar?
2 What do you do in the lessons?
3 And what do you do then?
4 Do you like the college?

2 Language Practice (C1.2)

A Write the questions and the answers.

Example: **1 Q:** Does she like the college?
            A: Yes, she likes the college.

1 college – the – does – like – she? (Yes)
2 Ricardo – come – does – Spain – from? (Yes)
3 what – time – classes – end – do? (3.30)
4 disco – Elisabeth – go – a –does – to – when? (at the weekend)
5 Mrs – do – White – talk – Mr – Elisabeth – to – and? (Yes)

B Write the questions for these answers.

Example: **1** *Do you have a brother or a sister?*

1 Yes, I have one brother and two sisters.
2 Yes, she has a Ford.
3 Yes, he watches television.
4 Yes, Ricardo likes the college.
5 Yes, we work on Saturday.

3 🎧 Speaking and Pronunciation (C1.1, 1.2, 2.1, 2.4)

A Listen and repeat.

Do you ... /dju: /
Do you go to work? /dju: gəʊ tə wɜːk/

Now listen and repeat the questions.

B Work with a partner. Ask the questions.

	Mon-Fri	Sat	Sun
1 What time do you get UP in the morning?			
2 Do you have BREAKfast?			
3 Do you go to WORK, or COLlege?			
4 What TIME do you go to work/college?			
5 Do you LIKE your work/college?			
6 Where do you have LUNCH?			
7 When do you go HOME from work/college?			
8 What time do you have DINner?			
9 What do you do in the EVEning?			
10 What time do you go to BED?			

C Write your partner's answers in ten sentences.

4 Vocabulary and Pronunciation

A In the classroom (C2.6)

1 Write the words.

1 a p _ _
2 a p _ _ _ _ _
3 a r _ _ _ _
4 a s _ _ _ _ _ _
5 a r _ _ _ _ _
6 a h _ _ _ - p _ _ _ _
7 a f _ _ _
8 an e _ _ _ _ _ _ _ b _ _ _
9 a c _ _ _ _ _ b _ _ _
10 p _ _ _ _
11 a d _ _ _ _ _ _ _ _
12 a d _ _ _
13 a c _ _ _ _

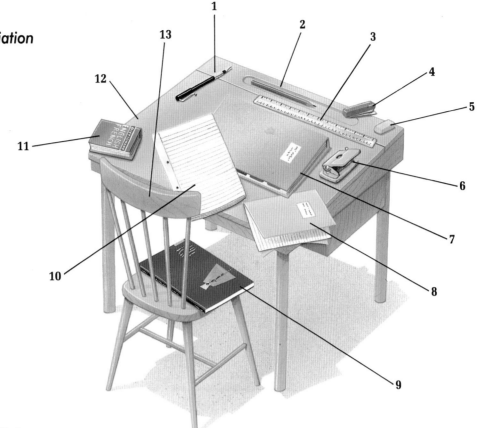

2 Mark the stress. **Example:** a <u>dic</u>tionary

B Learning English (C4)

Practise in groups of four. Student A is Elisabeth. Student B is Elena. Student C is Ricardo. And Student D is the teacher.

1 *Elisabeth:* Elena, where's the

.... ?

Elena: Sorry? I don't understand.

2 *Elena:* What's this in English?

Teacher: It's ....

3 *Ricardo:* Can I have the .... ?

Elisabeth: Sorry? I don't ....

4 *Elena:* .... this in English?

Teacher: It's a ....

5 *Teacher:* Look it up in the dictionary.

Ricardo: Sorry? I ....

6 *Ricardo:* .... in English?

Elisabeth: It's a ....

C Ask your teacher: What's this in English?

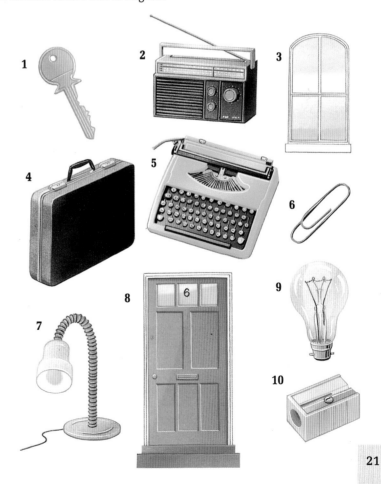

C Language Study

1 GRAMMAR

1.1 Verb form: The Present Simple

I	**come**	from Madrid.
You	**work**	on Saturday.
He	**read** s	the newspapers on Sunday.
She	**like** s	her English teacher.
We	**watch**	television in the evening.
They	**walk**	to school.

Irregular verbs

have

| I
You
We
They | **have** | lunch at one. |
| He/She/It | **has** | dinner at eight. |

go

| I
You
We
They | **go** | to work at nine. |
| He/She/It | **goes** | out to discos. |

do

| I
You
We
They | **do** | homework in the evening. |
| He/She/It | **does** | lots of things. |

watch

| I
You
We
They | **watch** | television. |
| He/She/It | **watches** | |

Use the Present Simple for

1 routines: things that happen every day, etc.
2 feelings: e.g. *'I like...'* and opinions: e.g. *'I think it's good.'*

1.2 Present Simple: Questions

Yes/No questions with the verb *to do*:

'**Do** you **work** on Saturday?' 'Yes.'
'**Do** German children **have** lunch at school?' 'No.'

NB: he/she/it – Mr White **work** s at home.

'**Do es** Mr White **work** at college?' 'No.'

Wh- questions with the verb *to do*:

1	2	3	4	
What When What time Where	**do** **does** **do** **do**	you Elisabeth children you	**do** **watch** **go** **have**	there? television? to school? lunch?

With the verb *to be* (page 10):

1	2	3	
What How old Where	is is is	the time? Richard? the cake?	(What's the time?) (Where's the cake?)

1.3 Adverb: *too*

Elisabeth goes to college. Elena goes to college.
= Elisabeth goes to college **and** Elena goes to college **too**.

1.4 Prepositions

for the children

Where? **at** the airport
at the camping site
at home/work/school/college
(NOT: at ~~the~~ home, at ~~the~~ work, at ~~the~~ school)
to the airport/a disco
to bed/**to** school
(NOT: to ~~the~~ bed, to ~~the~~ work, ~~to the~~ home)

When? **at** eight **o'clock**
in the **evening/morning/afternoon**
at night
after lunch/class
on Wednes**day**/Satur**day** etc.

1.5 Conjunctions: *or, but, then*

'Are you English **or** American?' 'I'm English.'

Grammar is difficult **but** it's useful.

I have breakfast, **then** I walk to college with Elena.

2 VOCABULARY

2.1 Routine (verbs)

to get up /get ʌp/
to go to work /gəʊ tə wɛ:k/
to go to school /gəʊ tə sku:l/
to walk /wɔ:k/

to watch (television) /wɒtʃ/
to go to bed /gəʊ tə bed/
to go out /aʊt/

to say /seɪ/
to read /ri:d/
to talk /tɔ:k/
to start /stɑ:t/

to end /end/
to have /hæv/ – a shower/a bath
               – breakfast/lunch/
                 dinner

come /kʌm/

2.2 Adjectives

nice /naɪs/
lovely /lʌvlɪ/
good /gʊd/

difficult /dɪfɪkəlt/
useful /ju:sfəl/

2.3 The day

the morning /'mɔ:nɪŋ/
the afternoon /'ɑ:ftənu:n/
the evening /'i:vnɪŋ/

2.4 The days of the week

Monday /'mʌndeɪ/	Friday /'fraɪdeɪ/
Tuesday /'tju:zdeɪ/	Saturday /'sætədeɪ/
Wednesday /'wenzdeɪ/	Sunday /'sʌndeɪ/
Thursday /'θɜ:zdeɪ/	

2.5 Occupations

an accountant /ə'kaʊntənt/   a student /'stju:dənt/

2.6 The classroom

a pen /pen/
a pencil /'pensəl/
a rubber /'rʌbə/
a ruler /'ru:lə/
a desk /desk/
a chair /tʃeə/
a course book /kɔ:s bʊk/

a stapler /'steɪplə/
a file /faɪl/
an exercise book /'eksəsaɪz bʊk/
paper /'peɪpə/
a hole-punch /həʊl pʌntʃ/
a dictionary /'dɪkʃənrɪ/

2.7 The home

a bathroom /'bɑ:θru:m/
a bedroom /'bedru:m/
a dining room /'daɪnɪŋ ru:m/
a kitchen /'kɪtʃɪn/

a living room /'lɪvɪŋ ru:m/
a study /'stʌdɪ/
a garden /'gɑ:dən/
a television /telɪ'vɪʒən/
   or a TV /ti: vi:/

2.8 Meals

breakfast /'brekfəst/
lunch /lʌntʃ/

tea /ti:/
dinner /'dɪnə/

2.9 Places

a cinema /'sɪnəmə/
a college /'kɒlɪdʒ/
a disco /'dɪskəʊ/

a library /'laɪbri:/
a party /'pɑ:tɪ/

2.10 Countries and nationalities

Germany /'dʒɜ:mənɪ/
Spain /speɪn/

German /'dʒɜ:mən/
Spanish /'spænɪʃ/

3 SITUATIONS

3.1 Introductions

'How do you do.'   'Welcome to ...'

3.2 Conversation: Answers

'He works at home.'
'I see.'

'Is that OK?'
'That's fine.'

'Is this Jane's room?'
'Yes. That's right.'

3.3 Telling the time

'What's the time?'

'It's one o'clock.'   'It's eight o'clock.'

'It's half past one.'   'It's half past eight.'

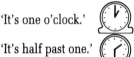

3.4 Permission

'You **can** have a shower any time.' 'Thank you.'

4 LEARNING ENGLISH

I don't understand.

Ask/Answer a question.

Draw a plan.

Write a sentence.

Mark the stress.

Listen and repeat.

A *The King's Hotel, Edinburgh*

1 Reading and Language Practice (C1.2)

Look at the information about these hotels and
write the sentences.

The King's Hotel	310 rooms	🍴		📺		in City Centre
The Airport Hotel	34 rooms		≋		🌹	City Centre 15km

1 The King's Hotel is near the centre of Edinburgh. The Airport Hotel .... near
   the centre of Edinburgh.
2 The King's Hotel has a restaurant. The Airport Hotel .... a restaurant.
3 The King's Hotel .... a swimming pool. The Airport Hotel has a swimming pool.
4 The King's Hotel .... a garden. The Airport Hotel has a garden.
5 The King's Hotel has a television. The Airport Hotel .... a television.

2 📟 Listening and Reading

Listen and read.

Receptionist: Can I help you?
Luigi: Yes – my name's Luigi Zambelli.
Receptionist: Oh, yes – Mr Zambelli. Welcome to Edinburgh. Are you here for the
                Festival?
Luigi: Yes, I am. I'm a journalist with a magazine ... in Italy.
Receptionist: That's interesting. Here we are – a single room with a shower.
Luigi: Yes, that's right.
Receptionist: Here's your key, Room 86. And ... information about the hotel.
Luigi: Thank you. Oh – can I telephone Italy from my room?
Receptionist: No, I'm sorry. You can't. You can phone from over there.
Luigi: And does the hotel have a fax?
Receptionist: Yes, it does.
Luigi: Good. Thank you.

3 Speaking (C2.1)

Practise with a partner. Ask and answer questions. Student A turn to page 125.
Student B turn to page 127.

4 Reading and Language Practice (C1.3 and 2.1)

Look at the information about the hotel and answer Luigi's questions. Use short answers.

Examples: *'Is the hotel near the cinemas   'Yes, it is.'*
and theatres?'
'When is lunch?'   'From 12 noon to 2.30.'

1 Is the hotel in the city centre?
2 Does the hotel have a fax?
3 Does the hotel have room service?
4 Does the hotel have a garden?
5 Can I change money at the hotel?
6 Can I buy theatre tickets at the hotel?
7 When is breakfast?
8 When does the Change Counter open?
9 Where can I buy postcards?
10 When can I buy stamps?
11 Where can I buy a book about Edinburgh?

THE KING'S HOTEL ★★★★★

* In the centre of Edinburgh, near the cinemas and theatres, the King's Hotel is perfect for the visitor to the Edinburgh Festival.
* Meal times in the Royal Restaurant:
  Breakfast - from 7.30am to 10.00am
  Lunch - from 12 noon to 2.30pm
  Dinner - from 6.00pm to 12 midnight
  Room Service 24 hours a day - telephone 124
* At the Hotel Change Counter you can change money or traveller's cheques - open from 9.00am to 5.00pm.
* At the Hotel Ticket Office you can buy tickets for the festival films, plays and concerts - open from 9.00am to 7.00pm.
* The Hotel Shop sells postcards, stamps, telephone cards and guide books - open from 8.00am to 8.00pm.
* International telephone calls and fax - ask in Reception.

5 Speaking

Now ask and answer the questions in Exercise 4 with a partner. Student A is Luigi. Student B is the receptionist.

6 Language Practice and Pronunciation (C1.1 and 3.3)

Can I have *two tickets* for *Macbeth* for *Monday, please*?

Practise saying the sentence.
Now use these words: *one/Hamlet/tomorrow*
three/Othello/today
two/the Tempest/tonight

B Telephoning home

1 Listening and Writing (C3.4 and 3.5)

Listen and write.

Assistant:	**Can I** .... you?
Luigi:	**Can I have** a .... card please?
Assistant:	Anything else?
Luigi:	No, ... all, thank you.

Luigi:	**Can I** .... Italy?
Assistant:	Yes, from the .... over there.
Luigi:	Thank you.
Joanna:	Pronto ...
Luigi:	Hello, it's ....
Joanna:	Oh, hi. How .... you?
Luigi:	Fine – everything's fine. How are .... ? And the .... ?
Joanna:	We're OK.

2 Reading (C2.2)

Look at the phone book and answer these questions.

1 What is the international code for Italy?
2 What is the number for Florence?
3 What is the number for Rome?
4 The time in Scotland is 3.00pm. What is the time in Italy?
5 You want the operator. What number do you phone?

Italy

International code **010**	Followed by country code **39**	Followed by area code listed below

Bari **80**	Modena **59**	Rome **6**
Bologna **51**	Naples **81**	Salerno **89**
Bolzano **471**	Padua **49**	San Remo **184**
Brescia **30**	Palermo **91**	Sassari **79**
Cagliari **70**	Parma **521**	Siracusa **931**
Capri **81**	Perugia **75**	Taranto **99**
Catania **95**	Pescara **85**	Terni **744**
Como **31**	Piacenza **523**	Trieste **40**
Florence **55**	Pisa **50**	Turin **11**

Operator Services 155 Directory Inquiries 153
Time difference **1** hour later than GMT

3 Pronunciation and Listening

1 Listen and say these phone numbers.

01 34 79   141 27859   23 41 09
047 3423   21 38 44

2 Now listen and write the numbers.

a ....
b ....
c ....
d ....
e ....

3 Practise with a friend:
What's your phone number?

4 Study Skills: Vocabulary

Use a dictionary.

pronunciation   grammar   meaning

hotel /həʊ'tel/ *n.* where you can buy a meal and have a bedroom

ticket /'tɪkɪt/ *n.* a paper you buy to go on a train or bus or to go to the cinema or the theatre

A spidergram can help you learn vocabulary:

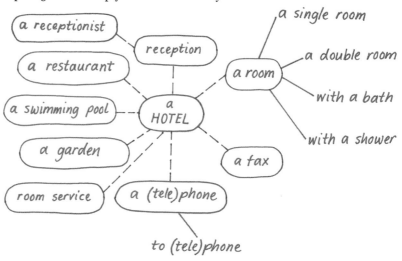

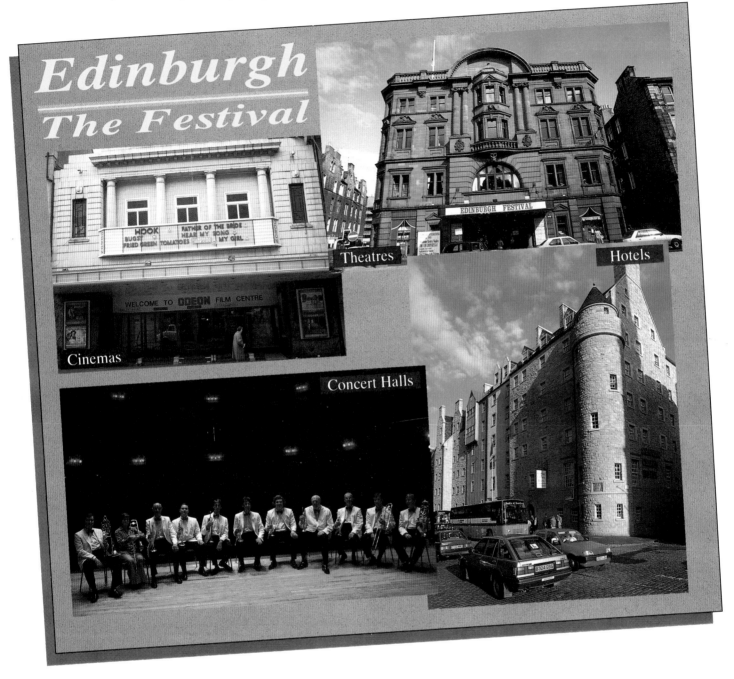

Use your dictionary. Look at the photographs. Now put these words in four groups.

a hotel	a restaurant	a concert hall	a film	a play	a concert
an orchestra	a ticket	a receptionist	a double room	a shower	
a film star	an actor	a programme	a cinema	a theatre	

6 🎦 Pronunciation

A Use your dictionary. Where is the stress on these words?

shower   hotel   concert   programme   ticket   actor

Which word is different?

B The pronunciation of *not* is /nɒt/. The pronunciation of *no* is /nəʊ/. Listen to these words. Do you hear the sound /ɒ/ or /əʊ/?

hotel	open	Scotland
phone	job	shop
concert	go	postcard

C Language Study

1 GRAMMAR

1.1 Modal verb *can* /kæn/

1	2	3
I	can	
You	can	
He	can	
She	can	verb
We	can	
They	can	

Example: Luigi **can** buy tickets at the hotel.

Negative

cannot (**can't**) /kɑ:nt/

I	can't	fax	from home.
You	can't	phone	from your room.

Question

Can	I	buy	tickets at the hotel?
Can	he	telephone	Italy?

1.2 Present Simple: Negative (do/does + not)

don't /dəʊnt/   doesn't /'dʌzənt/

1	2	3
I	do not (don't)	have a single room.
You	do not (don't)	work on Saturday.
He/She	does not (doesn't)	go to school.
The hotel	does not (doesn't)	have a garden.
We	do not (don't)	have a phone in our room.
They	do not (don't)	have a television.

1.3 Short answers

Does the hotel have a fax?	Yes, it **does**.
Does the hotel have a garden?	No, it **doesn't** (does not).
Does Luigi come from Italy?	Yes, he **does**.
Do the children go to school on Wednesday?	Yes, they **do**.
Do they go to school on Saturday?	No, they **don't** (do not).
Can I buy a phonecard here?	Yes, you **can**.
Can he buy plane tickets at the hotel?	No, he **can't** (cannot)

1.4 The Indefinite Article: *a/an* with jobs

'What do you do?'
'I'm **a** journalist. / I'm **a** photographer. / I'm **an** accountant.'

Notice the pronunciation – **a** /ə/ **an** /ən/

1.5 Adjectives

a **fine**¹ day²

an **interesting**¹ book²

'How are you?' 'I'm **fine**.'
'I'm a journalist.' 'That's **interesting**.'

1.6 Prepositions

information **about** the hotel

from 7.30 **to** 10.00

2 VOCABULARY

2.1 A hotel

Reception /rɪ'sepʃən/
a receptionist /rɪ'sepʃənɪst/
a single room /'sɪŋgəl ru:m/
a double room /'dʌbl ru:m/
with a shower /wɪð ə 'ʃaʊə/
with a bath /wɪð ə bɑ:θ/

Describing a hotel

It **has** a restaurant/a shop/a garden/a swimming pool/ room service.

2.2 Telephoning

a telephone /'teləfəʊn/
a phone /fəʊn/ } nouns

to telephone /'teləfəʊn/
to phone /fəʊn/ } verbs

a telephone book /'teləfəʊn bʊk/
a phonecard /'fəʊnkɑ:d/
the operator /ðɪ 'ɒpəreɪtə/
a telephone number /'teləfəʊn 'nʌmbə/
a code /kəʊd/

2.3 People

a journalist /'dʒɜ:nəlɪst/
a receptionist /rɪ'sepʃənɪst/
a baby /'beɪbɪ/

2.4 Countries and nationalities

Italy /ˈɪtəlɪ/   Italian /ɪˈtæljən/
Scotland /ˈskɒtlənd/   Scots /skɒts/

international /ɪntəˈnæʃənəl/

2.5 On holiday

a postcard /ˈpəʊstkɑːd/
a stamp (for Italy) /stæmp/
a guide book /ˈgaɪd bʊk/

2.6 Entertainment

a cinema /ˈsɪnəmə/
a film /fɪlm/
a theatre /ˈθɪətə/
a play /pleɪ/
a concert hall /ˈkɒnsət hɔːl/
a concert /ˈkɒnsət/
a magazine /mægəˈziːn/
a ticket /ˈtɪkɪt/
a programme /ˈprəʊgræm/
a festival /ˈfestɪvəl/

2.7 Money

a traveller's cheque /ˈtrævələz tʃek/
to buy /baɪ/
to sell /sel/
to change /tʃeɪndʒ/

2.8 Talking about time

today /təˈdeɪ/
tonight /təˈnaɪt/
tomorrow /təˈmɒrəʊ/

3 SITUATIONS

3.1 Permission

'You **can** phone from over there.' 'Thank you.'

3.2 Offering

'**Can** I help you?'

'You **can** change money at the hotel.'

3.3 Requesting

'**Can I have** a ticket for tonight, please?'
'**Can I have** a phonecard, please?'
'**Can** we buy stamps at the hotel?'

3.4 At the shop

'Can I have | a phonecard
a postcard
a guide book
three stamps | please?'

'Anything else?'
'No, that's all, thank you.'

3.5 Conversation

'Hi, how are you?'

'Fine, thanks. How are *you*?'

'Fine.'

A George and Barbara from Boston, USA

1 Reading

A George and Barbara are from Boston in the United States of America. They are visitors on a house exchange in Brighton in the south of England. Read the letter from Mike and Julia, the owners of the house in Brighton.

9 Queens Road
Brighton
Sussex

Dear George and Barbara,
Welcome to England, and welcome to Brighton!
Here is some information to help you:
The neighbours – Pauline and Martin at number 11, and
Ian and Margo at number 7 – are very nice. Get the
house keys from Ian and Margo.
There are instructions for the microwave oven, the
dishwasher and the washing machine in the kitchen. Look
in the drawer under the oven.
There are instructions for the video in the living
room. Look on top of the television.
The vacuum cleaner is in the cupboard under the stairs.
There's a map of the town on the desk in the study and a
guide book on the bookshelf near the big English dictionary.
The car keys are on the kitchen table, but don't drive into
the town centre. Parking is difficult and expensive. Go by bike –
the bikes are in the garage.
Please look after Tabitha for us – she sleeps in the garage
and the cat food is in the cupboard opposite the fridge.
Don't put her food in the garden – the neighbour's cat eats it!
The garden furniture is in the shed.
Have a good holiday and don't forget – send us a postcard!
Best wishes
Mike and Julia

B Where are they?

1 the keys
2 instructions for the dishwasher
3 the map
4 instructions for the video
5 the guide book
6 the car keys
7 the bikes
8 the vacuum cleaner
9 the garden furniture
10 the cat food

2 Speaking

Work in pairs. Student A look at page 126. Student B look at page 128.

3 Language Practice (C1.1)

A Read the letter in Exercise 1 again and write down the verbs in the imperative (orders).

B Match the sentences to the pictures.

1 Come and see me at half past three.
2 Practise!
3 Put it over there, please.
4 Read this!
5 Say 'thank you'!
6 Write your name here.

c

b

f

a

d

e

4 Listening

Listen to the instructions.

Example: 1 *Say 'good morning' in your language.*

Bonjour   Guten Morgen   Buenos Dias   Buongiorno   お早うございます。

B The town of Brighton

1 ▣ Listening

George and Barbara are in the town of Brighton for the first time. They ask someone the way four times. Listen and look at the map. What number are these places on the map?

a   the theatre
b   the Hotel Metropole
c   the market
d   the museum

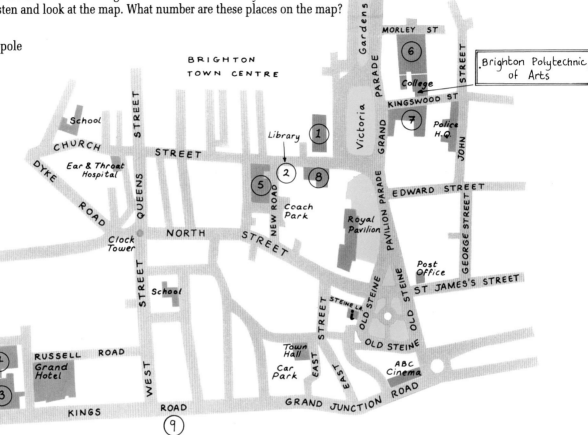

2 Reading and Language Practice (C1.3 and 1.4)

Read the note from Mike and Julia about the shops. Write in the missing words.

on the left	near	along	turn right	to	turn left

PS
Brighton town centre is very nice, but there are some
good shops (1) _____ here too. This is the way – go out of
our house, (2) _____ and walk (3) _____ our
road (4) _____ Sussex Road. Then (5) _____ and
go (6) _____ Sussex Road. (7) _____ and take
the second (8) _____. There are a lot of shops
in this road. Here is a map.

3 Vocabulary and Language Practice (C1.4, 2.1, 2.3)

Write ten sentences about the places and shops in this street:

the baker's	the chemist's
a restaurant	a shoe shop
a newsagent's	the bank
a supermarket	the greengrocer's
the butcher's	the hairdresser's

Example: *The first shop on the right is the butcher's.*

4 Pronunciation and Study Skills (C4.2)

A Listen and repeat. What sound comes in every word?

1 welcome /ˈwelkəm/
2 information /ɪnfəˈmeɪʃən/
3 neighbour /ˈneɪbə/
4 machine /məˈʃiːn/
5 cinema /ˈsɪnəmə/
6 cupboard /ˈkʌbəd/
7 dictionary /ˈdɪkʃənrɪ/
8 garden /ˈgɑːdən/
9 furniture /ˈfɜːnɪtʃə/
10 opposite /ˈɒpəsɪt/

B Listen again and <u>underline</u> the stressed syllable in each of the words. What sound is *not* underlined each time?

5 Speaking

A **Asking the way**

You are at the car park near the town hall.

A: Excuse me. Can you tell me the way to the cinema?
B: Yes, of course. Go along East Street to Grand Junction Road. Turn left along Grand Junction Road and the cinema's on the left.
A: OK ... I go along East Street to Grand Junction Road. I turn left along Grand Junction Road and the cinema's on the left. Thank you!
B: You're welcome!

Now you. Practise with a partner. Look at the map of Brighton and ask (and tell) the way from the car park near the town hall to:

1 the hospital
2 the Royal Pavilion
3 the police station
4 the Tourist Information Centre

B Work with a partner. Student A look at the instructions on page 127. Student B look at page 129.

C Language Study

1 GRAMMAR

1.1 Verb form: The Imperative

Use the imperative for orders – to tell someone to do something.

Verb	Imperative	Negative Imperative
to look	Look!	Don't look!
to listen	Listen!	Don't listen!
to drive	Drive!	Don't drive!
to turn	Turn (right)!	Don't turn (right)!

1.2 Object pronouns

Subject pronouns	Object pronouns
I (*I live in Oxford.*)	me (*Tell me the way.*)
we (*We watch television.*)	us (*Send us a postcard.*)

1.3 Prepositions

Where? under (the table)
on top of (the television) /ɒn tɒp əv/
into (the car park)
opposite (the bank)
near (the bank)
to (the museum)

Direction: from (the neighbours)

along (the road)

1.4 Adverbs

Where? right /raɪt/

on your right

left /ləft/

on your left

in the south /saʊθ/

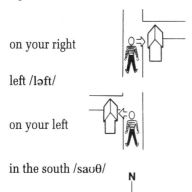

2 VOCABULARY

2.1 Ordinal numbers

1st	first	6th	sixth
2nd	second	7th	seventh
3rd	third	8th	eighth
4th	fourth	9th	ninth
5th	fifth	10th	tenth

2.2 Electrical machines

a dishwasher /'dɪʃwɒʃə/
a microwave /'maɪkrəʊweɪv/
a video /'vɪdɪjəʊ/
a vacuum cleaner /'vækjuːm 'kliːnə/
a fridge /frɪdʒ/
an oven /'ʌvən/

for the machines:
instructions /ɪn'strʌkʃənz/

2.3 Places and shops in town

the baker's /'beɪkəz/
the bank /bænk/
the butcher's /'bʊtʃəz/
a car park /kɑː pɑːk/
the chemist's /'kemɪsts/
a cinema /'sɪnəmə/
a clock tower /klɒk 'taʊwə/
a coach park /'kəʊtʃ pɑːk/
the greengrocer's /'griːngrəʊsəz/
a hospital /'hɒspɪtəl/
a market /'mɑːkɪt/
a museum /mjuː'ziːəm/
the newsagent's /'njuːzeɪdʒənts/
a police station /pə'liːs 'steɪʃən/
a post office /pəʊst 'ɒfɪs/
a railway station /'reɪlweɪ 'steɪʃən/
a road (West Road) /rəʊd/
a shoe shop /ʃuː ʃɒp/
a sports centre /spɔːts 'sentə/
a street (Oxford St) /striːt/
a theatre /'θɪətə/

2.4 In a house

a cat /kæt/
a bookshelf /'bʊkʃelf/
a drawer /drɔː/
food /fuːd/
house exchange /haʊs ɪks'tʃeɪndʒ/
an owner /'əʊnə/
a shed /ʃed/

2.5 Transport

(by) bicycle (cycle, bike) /ˈbaɪsɪkəl, ˈsaɪkəl, baɪk/
(by) coach /kəʊtʃ/
the railway /ˈreɪlweɪ/

2.6 Adjectives

expensive /ɪkˈspensɪv/

big /bɪg/

small /smɔ:l/

2.7 Verbs

to go shopping /ˈʃɒpɪŋ/
to forget /fəˈget/
to drive /draɪv/
to send /send/

3 SITUATIONS

3.1 Asking the way

'Excuse me. Can you tell me the way to the cinema, please?'

3.2 Responding to thanks

'Thanks.' 'You're welcome!'

4 LEARNING ENGLISH

to look up (a word in a dictionary)
to underline (a word)

4.1 Writing letters in English

A letter to a friend:

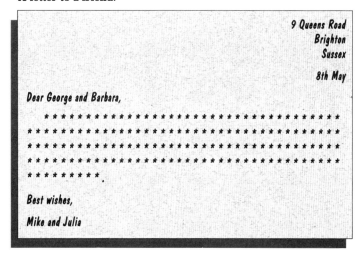

4.2 Pronunciation

Word stress

A word has one, two, three, or more syllables:

One syllable words: yes car shoe road
Two syllable words: garden (gar-den) welcome (wel-come)
                          baker (ba-ker) police (po-lice)
Three syllable words: cinema (ci-ne-ma) opposite (op-po-site)
                          hospital (ho-spi-tal)

Words with two or more syllables have a **stressed** syllable and one or more **unstressed** syllables:

	Stressed syllable		
	GAR	– den	
	WEL	– come	
	BA	– ker	
po –	LICE		
	CI	– ne	– ma
	HO	– spi	– tal

Unstressed syllables often have the sound /ə/:

	GAR	– den		/gɑ:	– dən/	
	WEL	– come		/wel	– kəm/	
	BA	– ker		/beɪ	– kə/	
po –	LICE		/pə –	li:s/		
HO	– spi	– tal		/hɒ	– spɪ	– təl/

UNIT 6 DR LI FROM HONG KONG

A At the hospital

1 Listening and Speaking

A Listen and read.

Dr Farmer: Welcome to Addenbrookes, Dr Li. This is Dr Manning.
Dr Manning: How do you do?
Dr Li: How do you do?
Dr Farmer: And this is Nurse Duffy.
Nurse Duffy: How do you do?
Dr Li: Pleased to meet you.

Now you. Practise in groups of four.

B Dr Manning shows Dr Li the hospital. Look at the plan and listen. Where do they go?

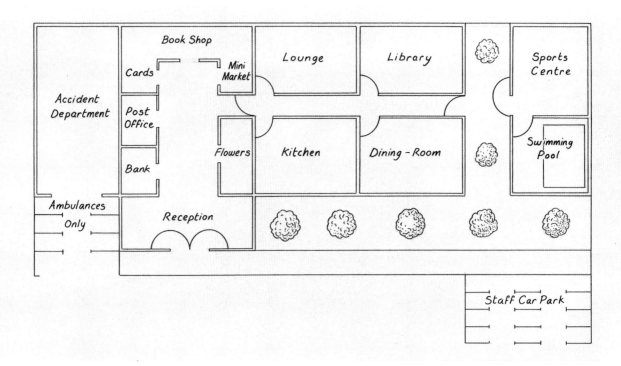

2 Vocabulary

Where can Dr Li ...
have lunch?
read the newspapers?
borrow books?
buy books?
swim?
play squash?

3 Reading and Language Practice (C1.1)

Read this information about cycling and complete the sentences.

1 You .... have lights at night.
2 You .... cycle on the right.
3 You .... stop when the traffic lights are red.
4 You .... have a bell.
5 You .... cycle on the pavement.

Cycle on the left – and **don't** cycle on the pavement.

Use a bell.

TRING!

Use lights at night.

Stop when the lights are red.

4 Language Practice (C1.1)

Write a sentence under the pictures **1** to **5**.
Use *musn't*.

Example:

EMERGENCY ENTRANCE
AMBULANCES ONLY
NO PARKING

1 *You musn't park here.*

2 _____

3 _____

SILENCE

4 _____

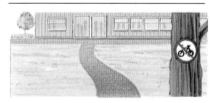

5 _____

5 Speaking and Writing

Work with a partner and complete the letter from Dr Li to his friend, George. Student A turn to page 131. Student B turn to page 129.

6 ⌨Pronunciation

These words have the sound /ɜː/ or /ʌ/.
Listen – do you hear sound /ɜː/ or /ʌ/?

son	country	girl	mother
number	word	lunch	work
journalist	money	nurse	lovely

B An accident

1 ⊞Listening and Vocabulary (C2.1, 2.2, 2.4)

Listen, then label the pictures. Use these words.

telephone	ambulance	police car	bicycle	truck	policeman
sports bag	squash racquet	hospital	nurse	receptionist	patient

b

a

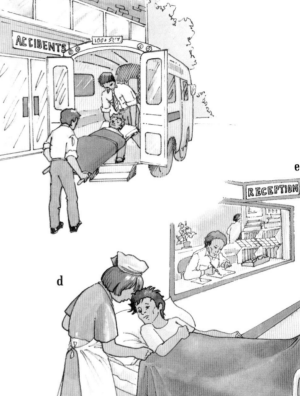

e

c

d

2 ⊞Listening

Listen, then answer the questions.

Dr Li: Hello, Simon Hebden?
Simon: Yes.
Dr Li: OK. Now – let's see. It's your arm, isn't it?
Simon: Yes.
Dr Li: Mmm – does that hurt?
Simon: Yes, and my leg hurts too...

Dr Li: Don't worry. He's OK. His arm's broken ... and his leg hurts but it isn't broken. You can't use your arm for about five weeks, and this mustn't get wet ... so be careful when you have a bath or a shower.
Simon: And I can't write – I'm left-handed!

3 Vocabulary and Speaking (C2.3)

A Label the picture with these words.

head	face	eye
nose	mouth	ear
arm	hand	leg
	foot	back

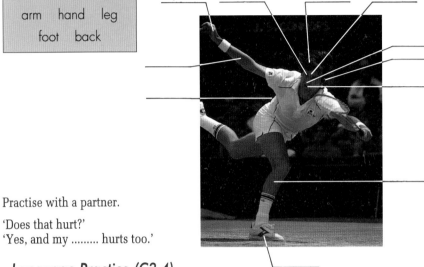

B Practise with a partner.

'Does that hurt?'
'Yes, and my .... hurts too.'

4 Language Practice (C3.4)

5 Study Skills

Look at these sentences. Do you think they are:

a about permission
b requesting
c offering
d about ability?

1 Can I help you?
2 Can you ride a bike?
3 You can park here.
4 Can I have two stamps for Hong Kong, please?
5 You can have a shower any time.
6 I can do that for you.
7 I can't write – my arm's broken.
8 Can you swim?
9 Can you write your name here, please?
10 He can read but he can't write.

How many sentences can you write about these people?

Example: *He can write but he can't play football.*

You can use these words.

write	speak	see	eat	hear	swim	walk	run	ride a bike
have a bath	play football	play squash	have a shower	play tennis				

C Language Study

1 GRAMMAR

1.1 Modal verb: *must* /mʌst/

	must	**verb**	
I You He She We They	***must***	**stop**	when the traffic lights are red.

Negative: *must not* (*mustn't*) /'mʌsənt/

You	***mustn't***	**smoke**	in the dining room.

1.2 Quantifier: *a lot of*

There are **a lot of** bicycles in Cambridge.
There are **a lot of** accidents.
There are **a lot of** people here.
There is **a lot of** furniture in the room.

2 VOCABULARY

2.1 At the hospital

a doctor /'dɒktə/
a nurse /nɜːs/
a patient /'peɪʃənt/
an ambulance /'æmbjʊləns/
an accident /'æksɪdənt/
to hurt /hɜːt/

2.2 At the Sports Centre

to play squash, tennis /skwɒʃ/ /'tenɪs/
a squash court /skwɒʃ kɔːt/
to swim /swɪm/

2.3 The body

a head /hed/
a face /feɪs/
an eye /aɪ/
a nose /nəʊz/
a mouth /maʊθ/
an ear /ɪə/
an arm /ɑːm/
a leg /leg/
a hand /hænd/
a foot /fʊt/
a back /bæk/

2.4 On the road

to cycle /'saɪkəl/
a truck /trʌk/
a police car /pə'liːs kɑː/
a pavement /'peɪvmənt/

a bell /bel/
a light /laɪt/
traffic lights /'træfɪk laɪts/

2.5 The library

to borrow /'bɒrəʊ/
a library card /'laɪbrɪ kɑːd/
a newspaper /'njuːzpeɪpə/
a librarian /laɪ'breərɪən/

2.6 Places

inside /ɪnsaɪd/
outside /aʊtsaɪd/
a university /juːnɪ'vɜːsɪtɪ/

2.7 People

everyone /'evrɪwʌn/
policeman /pə'liːsmən/

2.8 Adjectives

red /red/
wet /wet/
cold /kəʊld/
good /gʊd/
broken /'brəʊkən/
left-handed /left 'hændɪd/

2.9 Routine

to start /stɑːt/
to finish /'fɪnɪʃ/

3 SITUATIONS

3.1 Introductions

'This is Dr Li.'
'Pleased to meet you.'

3.2 Thanking

'Thank you very much.'

3.3 Obligation/Strong advice

You **must** have lights.
You **must** be careful.

Prohibition/Strong advice

You **mustn't** cycle on the pavement.
You **mustn't** worry.

3.4 Ability

I **can** swim and I **can** ride a bike.
He **can't** see and he **can't** hear.
Can you read and write in English?

3.5 Giving opinions – *think*

I	**think**	it	is	broken.
You	**think**	his name	is	Tom.
He	**thinks**	it	is	OK.
She	**thinks**	the cakes	are	45 pence.
We	**don't think**	he	is	in Edinburgh.
They	**don't think**	his leg	is	broken.

3.6 Conversation

4 LEARNING ENGLISH

to label

A People

1 Vocabulary

A 1 Which countries do these people come from?
   2 What languages do they speak?

Elizabeth Schaeffer

Marie Lebrun

George Baker

Ricardo Pedras

Luigi Zambelli

Tony Day

B Match the jobs with the sentences and choose *a* or *an*:

teacher accountant journalist actor doctor student receptionist photographer

1 He's a/an .... – he works in a bank.
2 She's a/an .... at the university.
3 A/An .... writes for a newspaper.
4 A/An .... works in the theatre.
5 A/An .... works in a hospital.
6 A/An .... works in a school.
7 She's a/an .... – she sells pictures to magazines.
8 He's a/an .... – he works in a hotel.

3 🔊 Listening

Look at the map and listen to the instructions.
Then answer the question at the end: *'Where are you?'*

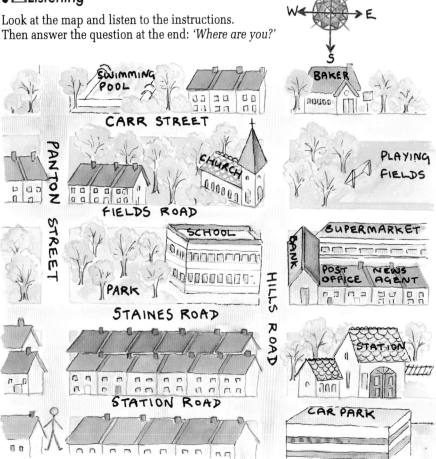

4 Speaking

Work in pairs. Student A look at page 131 and student B look at page 129.

5 Vocabulary

A Fill in the spidergram for the day.

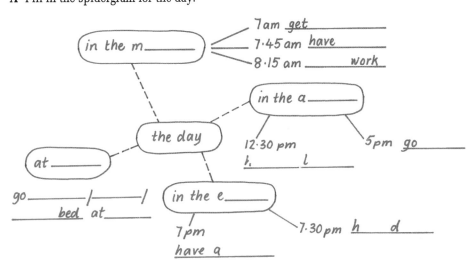

2 Language Practice

A Write the questions.

    Example: **1** *What time do you get up?*

    1 what time / get up?
    2 have / a brother or a sister?
    3 like / coffee?
    4 what countries / like / (for a holiday)?
    5 what / do? (what job?)
    6 where / work?
    7 what time / have / dinner?
    8 what / do / in the evening?
    9 what time / go / to bed?
    10 read / in bed?

B Work with a partner. Ask and answer the questions in Exercise 2A.

B Now draw a spidergram for *your* day (with times). Work with a partner and talk about your spidergram.

1 🎧 Dictation (20 marks)

Listen three times.

A Listen, but don't write.
B Listen again, and write what you hear.
C Listen, and read your writing.

2 Look at the things. Write the sentences. (12 marks)

Example: *It's Tony's bag. It's his bag.*

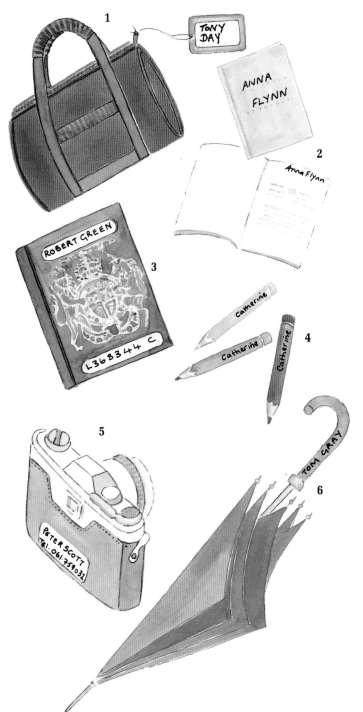

3 A Underline the stressed syllables of the words. (10 marks)

> ***Example:*** ac-<u>coun</u>-tant (accountant)

1 ac-ci-dent (accident)
2 ac-tor (actor)
3 Bri-tain (Britain)
4 dif-fe-rent (different)
5 ma-ga-zine (magazine)
6 a-long (along)
7 care-ful (careful)
8 break-fast (breakfast)
9 for-get (forget)
10 pho-to-gra-pher (photographer)

B Tick the syllable with the sound /ə/. (10 marks)

4 Here are the answers. What are the questions? (20 marks)

> ***Example:*** *At the weekend? I go to the disco or to the cinema.*
> **Question: What do you do at the weekend?**

1 'It's half past two.'
2 'That's my sister.'
3 'Her name's Angela.'
4 'Yes, this is my bag.'
5 'The restaurant? It's over there.'
6 'The watch? It's $68.'
7 'The English word for that? It's a vacuum cleaner.'
8 'Richard is six.'
9 'Yes, you can. How much money do you want to change?'
10 'Postcards? You can buy them at the post office.'

5 Where in the house (or outside) do you usually see these things? (16 marks)

1 a shower
2 a desk
3 a bed
4 a table and chairs
5 a microwave oven
6 a fridge
7 a shed
8 a video

6 You are going on holiday – by plane – to Britain from your country. Write *must*, *mustn't*, *can* or *can't* in the sentences. (12 marks)

1 You .... take your passport.
2 You .... forget your ticket.
3 You .... buy some films in the Duty-Free shop.
4 You .... take a lot of bags with you into the plane.
5 Sometimes you .... watch a film.
6 You .... listen to instructions.

C *Language Study*

The verb *to be*

I	am
he/she/it	is
you/we/they	are

The Present Simple

Use the Present Simple for:
1 routines (things you do every day): *I get up at ...*
2 feelings: *I like .../I want ...*
3 opinions: *I think ...*

Regular verbs

I/you/we/they	work
he/she/it	works

Irregular verbs

I/you/we/they	he/she/it
have	has
go	goes
do	does
watch	watches

Modal verbs: *can, must*

I/you/we/they	must
he/she/it	can

(NOT: ~~he cans~~)

Questions

1 *to be, can, must*

I am ...	Am I ...?
He is ...	Is he ...?
I can ...	Can I ...?
She can ...	Can she ...?
I must ...	
She must ...	

2 Simple Present: use *do/does*

You work ...	Do you work?
He works ...	Does he work?

Negative

1 *to be, can't, mustn't*

I am ...	I'm not ...
He is ...	He isn't ...
I can...	I can't ...
She can ...	She can't ...
I must ...	I mustn't ...
She must ...	She mustn't ...

2 Simple Present: use *do not (don't)* or *does not (doesn't)*

You work ...	You don't work ...
He works ...	He doesn't work ...

Short answers

1 *to be, can*

Are you...?	Yes, I am.
	No, I'm not.
Is he ...?	Yes, he is.
	No, he isn't.
Can I ...?	Yes, you can.
	No, you can't.

2 Simple Present: use *do/does*

Do you work?	Yes, I do.
	No, I don't.
Does he work?	Yes, he does.
	No, he doesn't.

The Imperative

Look!	Don't look!
Listen!	Don't listen!

Pronouns & Possessive Adjectives

Subject pronouns	Possessive adjectives	Object pronouns
I	my	me
you	your	you
he	his	him
she	her	her
it	its	it
we	our	us
they	their	them

Demonstrative pronouns

Singular:	this	that
Plural:	these	those

Nouns

Regular plurals: add *-s*

car – car[s]   room – room[s]

Irregular plurals

child – child[ren]   watch – watch[es]
bus – bus[es]   man – m[e]n

Apostrophe *'s*
John's son (NOT: ~~the son of John~~)

Articles: *a/an, the*

1 No article:
   at home/work/college
   to work/school/bed

2 with occupations:
   She's a teacher.
   He's an accountant.

Prepositions

Where? in, at, under, on, under, on top of, near, opposite
Where to? (*movement*) to (*not with* 'home'), into, from, along
When? at (8 pm), in (the morning), on (Saturday), after (lunch),
from (7.30) to (8.30)

from (France)   with (a partner)   (information) about (the hotel)

Adverbs

Where? here, (over) there, on the right/left, on your right/left,
in the south
Where to? (*movement*) right, left

Conjunctions

and, or, but, then

UNIT 7 THE NEW YORK MARATHON

A The Race

1 Listening and Language Practice (C1.5)

A Listen and mark the route of the New York Marathon.

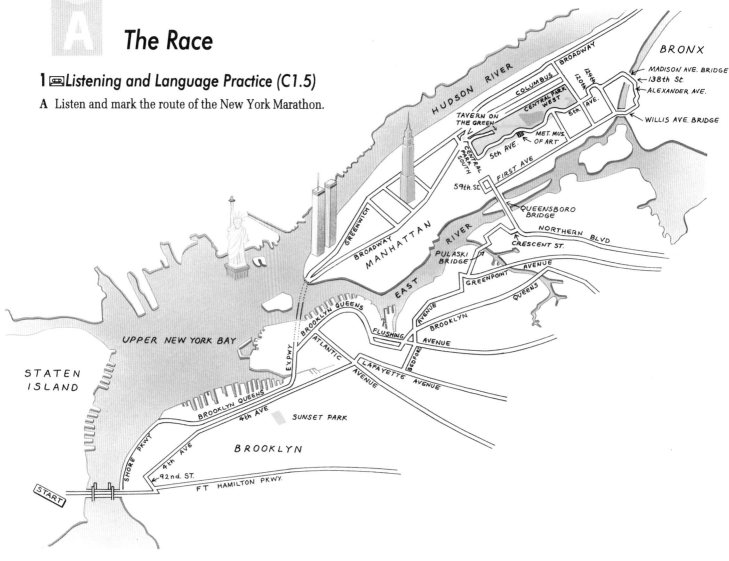

B Now underline the prepositions in the tapescript on page 135.

2 Reading and Vocabulary (C1.5)

Every day Ahmed runs 10 kilometres before breakfast. Look at the map. This is his route.

He goes (1) the (2), along the path, (3) the bridge, along the (4), (5) the railway, (6) the path, (7) the trees and back to his (8).

Write the words in the puzzle.

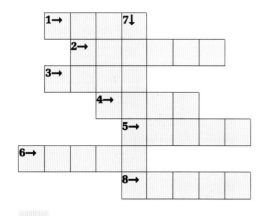

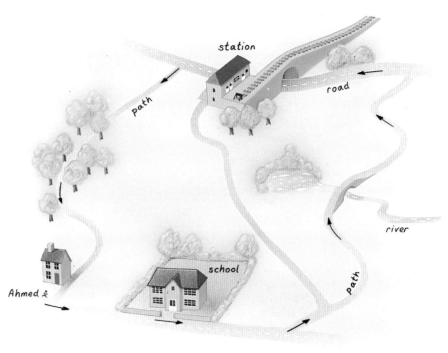

3 Reading

Match these newspaper headlines with the photographs.

a KENYAN WINS NEW YORK MARATHON

c NORWEGIAN WINS WOMEN'S RACE

b THOUSANDS RUN IN NEW YORK

d TIRED BUT HAPPY

e Thirsty Work

f 'MY LEGS HURT!'

B Runners

1 Reading and Vocabulary

A Read about Ahmed's day.

I get up at 6.30 every day and run 10 kilometres before breakfast. I have a shower, then I have breakfast with my wife and children – fruit, eggs, bread and milk. After breakfast I go to work – I'm a lawyer. I usually have a sandwich for lunch. After work I put on my tracksuit and running shoes and run 15 kilometres before dinner. For dinner we usually have chicken or fish with vegetables and rice. I drink milk or fruit juice. I don't like coffee or tea and I don't drink alcohol. After dinner I read a story to the children. In the evening I work or sometimes my wife and I go to the cinema. We usually go to bed at about 10.30 ...

B Use your dictionaries and look up the words for the fruit and the vegetables in the picture. Write the words and mark the stress.

C 1 Tick (✓) the things Ahmed eats.

   2 Tick (✓) the things Ahmed drinks.

What things do you eat and drink for breakfast? What food and drinks do you like? What don't you like?

2 Writing

Write about Ingrid Larsen, the winner of a women's marathon. Use these notes and start: *Ingrid gets up ...*

```
7.00 am – 6 kilometres
breakfast – husband
cereal, yoghurt, fruit juice
work – teacher
usually – salad – lunch
10 kilometres – dinner
vegetables, fish, eggs, rice, fruit
drink – fruit juice, tea
doesn't like – milk, coffee
read – watch television – sometimes – theatre
bed – 11.00 pm
```

3 Language Practice and Writing
(C1.1)

A Read the information and answer your teacher's questions.

Monday – Sunday

Every day he runs 20 kilometres.

He usually wears shorts or a tracksuit.

He drinks milk for breakfast.

Today he's running in the New York marathon - he's running 26 miles.

Today he's wearing red shorts and a number 12 on his back.

He's drinking a lot of water.

B Adam wants to go to the cinema. He phones his friends. What do they say?

1 *I'm sorry. I can't. I'm watching a film on TV.*
2 cook/dinner
3 paint/kitchen
4 look after/the children
5 study/for a test
6 *Oh yes! I want to see that film ...*

4 🔊 Pronunciation

Listen to the stress and put each word under the correct stress pattern.

| vegetable | yoghurt | cereal | sandwich | coffee | chicken | fruit | salad |
| bread | meat | banana | potato | tomato | pepper | apple | onion |

a ▮ b ▮▪ c ▮▪▪ d ▪▮▪

5 Speaking

Work in groups. What is your friend doing? Student A look at page 125, Student B look at page 127, Student C look at page 131, Student D look at page 130, Student E look at page 129, Student F look at page 128.

C Language Study

1 GRAMMAR

1.1 The Present Continuous

to be ...*ing*

I	**am**	
You	**are**	
He	**is**	studying.
She	**is**	
We	**are**	
They	**are**	

Negative

Today Ahmed is **not** (**isn't**) wearing his tracksuit.

'Yes/no' questions

1	2	3	4	5
They	are	running	over	the bridge.
Are	they	running	over	the bridge?

Wh- questions

What are you doing? (I'm **reading** a story.)

Where are we going? (We're going **to college**.)

Why are they walking now? (**Because** they are tired.)

NB: run → ru**nn**ing
get → ge**tt**ing
put → pu**tt**ing
have → having (*ø*)
write → writing (*é*)

1.2 *to like* + object

I	like	apples.
Ahmed	likes	fruit juice.
He/She	doesn't like	coffee.

(NOT: ~~He is liking milk.~~)

1.3 Adverbs of Frequency

We **usually** go to bed at 10.30.
or
Usually we go to bed at 10.30.

Monday	✓
Tuesday	✓
Wednesday	✓
Thursday	✓
Friday	✓
Saturday	
Sunday	✓

We **sometimes** go to the cinema.
or
Sometimes we go to the cinema.

DECEMBER					
Monday		6	13	20	27
Tuesday		7	14	21	28
Wednesday	1	8	15	22	29
Thursday	2	9	16	23	30
Friday	3	10	17	24	31
Saturday	4	11	18	25	
Sunday	5	12	19	26	

1.4 Nouns: Irregular Plural

Singular	Plural
man	men /men/
woman	women /'wɪmɪn/
person	people /'piːpəl/

1.5 Prepositions

Time

 Ahmed runs 15 kilometres **before** dinner.

 He reads a story **after** dinner.

} Dinner is at seven o'clock.

Movement

under the railway

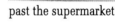

past the supermarket

over the bridge

through the trees

2 VOCABULARY

2.1 Food

to eat /i:t/

fruit /fru:t/
an apple /ˈæpəl/
a banana /bəˈnɑːnə/
grapes /greɪps/
a peach /pi:tʃ/
a pear /peə/

vegetables /ˈvedʒtəbəlz/
beans /bi:nz/
an onion /ˈʌnjən/
a pepper /ˈpepə/
a potato /pəˈteɪtəʊ/
a tomato /təˈmɑːtəʊ/

bread /bred/
cereal /ˈsɪərɪəl/
rice /raɪs/
a sandwich /ˈsændwɪtʃ/

chicken /ˈtʃɪkən/
fish /fɪʃ/
meat /mi:t/

cheese /tʃi:z/
an egg /eg/
salad /ˈsæləd/
yoghurt /ˈjɒgət/

2.2 Drinks

to drink /drɪŋk/
alcohol /ˈælkəhɒl/
coffee /ˈkɒfɪ/
fruit juice /fru:t dʒu:s/
milk /mɪlk/
tea /ti:/
water /ˈwɔːtə/

2.3 Clothes

to put on /pʊt ɒn/
to wear /weə/
shorts /ʃɔ:ts/
a tracksuit /ˈtræksu:t/

2.4 A Race

to run /rʌn/
the start /stɑ:t/
the finish /ˈfɪnɪʃ/
to win /wɪn/
the winner /ˈwɪnə/
a mile /maɪl/
a kilometre /ˈkɪləmi:tə, kɪˈlɒmɪtə/
to be in front /tə bi: ɪn frʌnt/
the route /ru:t/
a marathon /ˈmærəθən/

2.5 Numbers

hundreds of people (278 / 345 / 876) /ˈhʌndrədz/
thousands of runners (12,678 / 45,645) /ˈθaʊzəndz/

2.6 Jobs

a lawyer /ˈlɔɪjə/

2.7 Adjectives

happy /ˈhæpɪ/
hot /hɒt/
thirsty /ˈθɜːstɪ/
tired /ˈtaɪəd/

2.8 Countries and nationalities

Kenya /ˈkenjə/   Kenyan /ˈkenjən/
Norway /ˈnɔːweɪ/   Norwegian /nɔːˈwi:dʒən/

3 LEARNING ENGLISH

tick (✓)

notes

correct   4+4 = 8   ✓
          4+4 = 9   ✗ (not correct)

to study (for a test)

At the Bulgarian Stand

1 ☎Reading and listening (C2.1)

Frank Miller works for Primo Supermarkets, a big food company
in Britain. He is a buyer for his company, and he is visiting the
Food Fair in Frankfurt because he needs some new products.
Frank is looking at the food from different countries. He and his
friend Dorothea Lederer, a buyer from Germany, are talking to
Georg Vassilev from Bulgaria. Listen, then choose the correct
answers to the questions.

1 What food does Frank want to buy?

2 What time is the meeting?

2 Language Practice (C1.2 and 1.3)

A Put these pictures into two groups.

> *Example:* **Group 1** (We can count them) Picture **a**
> **Group 2** (We can't count it) Picture **d**

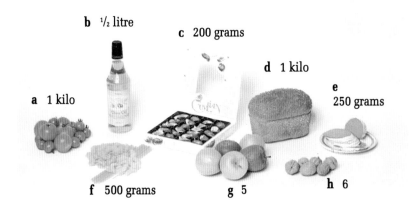

B Work with a partner. Ask *'How much ...?'* or *'How many ...?'*

> *Example:* **A:** *How many tomatoes are there?*
> **B:** *One kilo. How much pasta is there?*
> **A:** *Five hundred grams.*

3 Speaking (C3.1 and 3.2)

A Making suggestions

Practise with a partner. *A:* Let's have a drink.
B: OK. What about a cup of coffee?
A: OK.

Let's have	a drink. lunch. breakfast. dinner. tea.	What about	a cup of coffee? a cup of tea? some soup and a sandwich? an omelette and salad? some toast and honey? some fruit? an egg? some fish? some chicken? a piece of cake? a glass of milk? a bottle of water?

4 Speaking and Language Practice

Which country?

A Work with a partner. Take turns to make sentences with *have got.*

Examples: *They've got some delicious tomatoes in Italy.*
We've got some delicious oranges in Spain.

Use the names of the countries and these words:

tomatoes	chocolates	yoghurt	pasta	bread	cheese	grapes
oranges	apples	olive oil	walnuts	honey	liver sausage	

B What kind of food have you got in *your* country?

5 🔊 Vocabulary and Pronunciation

A Listen and repeat: ... of milk /əv mɪlk/
a bottle of milk

Now practise with a partner and match the words.

1	a bottle	of	chocolates
2	a glass	of	toast
3	a piece	of	orange juice
4	a box	of	tea
5	a cup	of	milk
6	a loaf	of	bread

B Listen and repeat: has got /əz gɒt/
Frank has got ...
Frank has got a box of
chocolates.

Now practise with a partner and make
sentences about the pictures with *has got.*

53

At the restaurant

1 📼*Listening and Speaking (C2.1)*

MENU

—•— **STARTERS** —•—
Tuna fish and tomato salad
Carrot and orange soup with bread
Chicken liver paté with toast

—•— **MAIN COURSES** —•—
(With baked potato or chips, and vegetables or salad)

— **Fish** —
Dover Sole
Scottish Salmon

— **Meat** —
Honey roast chicken
Steak and onion pie

— **Vegetarian** —
Walnut pie
Cheese or mushroom omelette

—•— **DESSERTS** —•—
Apple pie with cream
Baked bananas with ice-cream
Fruit salad with cream
Chocolate cheesecake

There is a British restaurant at the Food Fair. Frank, Dorothea and Georg are having lunch there.

A Listen. You are the waiter. Write down the orders.

Frank	Dorothea	Georg

B Role play

Work in groups of four – three customers and a waiter. Use the menu and order lunch.

Useful language

'What are you having?'
'What about you?'
'Honey roast chicken for me.'
'Let's have some coffee.'
'Can I have your order now, sir?'
'And for you, madam?'
'Have you got any Turkish coffee?'
'Can we have some water, please?'
'Waiter, can we see the menu again, please?'
'Can we have the bill, please?'
'What do you suggest?'

2 Language Practice (C1.3)

Make sentences for the pictures.

Examples:
1 *We've got a lot of vinegar but we haven't got much oil.*
2 *We've got a lot of apples but we haven't got many oranges.*

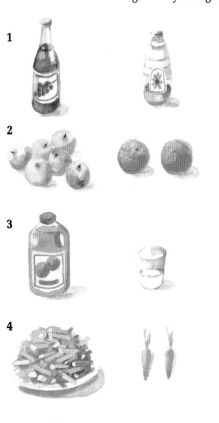

3 Reading and Speaking (C1.3)

A Read the recipe for Shopska Salad, a Bulgarian dish.

SHOPSKA SALAD

½ kilo tomatoes
2 large onions
350 grams sheep's cheese
1 green pepper
1 red pepper
1 cucumber

vinegar
salt & pepper
oil

Chop the vegetables and mix with the salt, pepper, oil and vinegar.

Grate the cheese over the salad.

B Work in pairs. Student A look at the recipe on this page. Student B look in the cupboard (page 130). Have you got everything you need? If not, make a shopping list.

Example:
A: *Have we got any tomatoes?*
B: *Yes, we have.*
A: *How many tomatoes have we got?*
B: *Half a kilo.*
A: *That's enough. We don't need any tomatoes.*
or
That's not enough. We need some tomatoes.

4 Reading and Writing

Frank Miller sends a fax to his company:

```
To:        John Waterstone, Buyer
Company:   Primo Supermarkets, Stevenage
From:      Frank Miller
Date:      14 April
Georg Vassilev from Bulgaria can sell us 400 kilos of sheep's
cheese a month at £4 a kilo. He has got some good walnuts to
sell too. Can we discuss an order for these? What do you
suggest – how many kilos, and at what price?
```

Now write a fax from Frank Miller about an order with Dorothea's company:

Dorothea Lederer – Germany – 400 kilos – liver sausage – £1.60 – tomatoes

C Language Study

1 GRAMMAR

1.1 The verb *have got*

You know the verb *have*. English people – when they speak – use *have got*, not *have*:

Examples: *Have you got any children?*
Yes, I have. I've got two sons.

Has he got a car?
No, he hasn't. But he's got a bike.

1.2 Nouns: Countable/Uncountable

Countable	Uncountable
tomatoes	bread (NOT: ~~breads~~)
oranges	milk
chocolates	cheese
apples	olive oil
a cucumber	a piece of bread (NOT: ~~a bread~~)

1.3 Talking about quantity

Countable	Uncountable
Have we got any apples?	Have we got any bread?
How many apples?	How much bread?
some apples	some bread
a lot of apples	a lot of bread

some/any

For **statements**, use *some*:

I've got some pasta.

For **negative statements** use *any*:

We haven't got any oranges or milk.

For asking **questions**, use *any*:

Have we got any oranges?
Are there any onions?
Is there any bread?

a lot of / not much/many

In the **affirmative**, use *a lot of*:

We've got a lot of bread.
You've got a lot of bananas.

In the **negative**, use *not much* (uncountable) or *not many* (countable):

We haven't got much milk. (uncountable)
You haven't got many apples. (countable)

How much? / How many?

Use *How much?* with **uncountable** nouns, and *How many?* with **countable** nouns:

How much bread is there?
How many apples are there?

2 VOCABULARY

2.1 At the restaurant

a starter /ˈstɑːtə/
the main course /meɪn kɔːs/
a dessert /dəˈzɜːt/
vegetarian /vedʒəˈteərɪən/
a waiter /ˈweɪtə/
'sir' /sɜː/
'madam' /ˈmædəm/
the menu /ˈmenjuː/
an order /ˈɔːdə/
the bill /bɪl/

2.2 Food and Cooking

to bake /beɪk/
to roast /rəʊst/

soup /suːp/
paté /ˈpæteɪ/
(liver) sausage /ˈlɪvə ˈsɒsɪdʒ/
toast /təʊst/
an omelette /ˈɒmlət/
peas /piːz/
vinegar /ˈvɪnɪgə/
olive oil /ˈɒlɪv ɔɪl/
mushrooms /ˈmʌʃruːmz/
pepper /ˈpepə/
salt /sɒlt/

honey /ˈhʌnɪ/
cheesecake /ˈtʃiːzkeɪk/
cream /kriːm/

2.3 How much is there?

a bottle of ... (milk) /ə ˈbɒtəl əv/
a cup of ... (tea) /ə kʌp əv/
a glass of ... (wine) /ə glɑːs əv/
a piece of ... (cake) /ə piːs əv/

a gram /græm/
a kilo (gram) /ˈkiːləʊ/
a litre /ˈliːtə/

2.4 Business – buying and selling

a buyer /ˈbaɪjə/
a company /ˈkʌmpənɪ/
a dollar /ˈdɒlə/
a (food/fashion) fair /feə/
a stand (at a fair) /stænd/
a product /ˈprɒdʌkt/
the price /praɪs/
an order /ˈɔːdə/

cauliflower /ˈkɒlɪflaʊə/
cucumber /ˈkjuːkʌmbə/
walnuts /ˈwɔːlnʌts/
pasta /ˈpæstə/
a loaf (of bread) /ləʊf/
pastry /ˈpeɪstrɪ/
pie /paɪ/

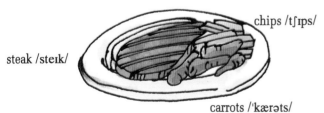

steak /steɪk/
chips /tʃɪps/
carrots /ˈkærəts/

chocolates /ˈtʃɒkləts/

2.5 Countries

Bulgaria /bʌlˈgeərɪə/   Bulgarian /bʌlˈgeərɪən/
Turkey /ˈtɜːkɪ/   Turkish /ˈtɜːkɪʃ/
Greece /griːs/   Greek /griːk/

2.6 Verbs

to count /kaʊnt/
to discuss /dɪsˈkʌs/
to know /nəʊ/
to need /niːd/
to suggest /səˈdʒest/
to taste /teɪst/

to make /meɪk/	to do /duː/
a cake	your homework
a salad	housework
a dress	a test
	an exercise

2.7 Adjectives

delicious /dɪˈlɪʃəs/
excellent /ˈeksələnt/
enough /ɪnˈʌf/
interested /ˈɪntrestɪd/
large /lɑːdʒ/
sure /ʃʊə/

green /griːn/   white /waɪt/

2.8 Miscellaneous

a month (noun) /mʌnθ/
a sheep (noun) /ʃiːp/
later (adverb) /ˈleɪtə/
because (conjunction) /bɪˈkɒz/

3 SITUATIONS

3.1 Suggestions: *Let's* .... (+ verb)

'Let's meet here at six o'clock.' 'Good idea!'

3.2 Offers: *What about* .... (+ noun)

'What about some coffee?' 'Yes, please.'

3.3 Requests and answers

'Can I take your order?'   'Of course.'
                               'Certainly.'

3.4 At the restaurant

See Useful Language on page 54.

A Jacquie Armstrong - Fashion Buyer

1 Vocabulary (C2.1-2.3)

A Use your dictionaries. Write the colours on the pencils.

B Find the words in your language for *cotton*, *wool*, *silk* and *leather*.

C What are the people wearing in Jacquie's drawing?

2 🔊 Listening and Study Skills (C2.1–2.3)

A Write the names next to the people in the photographs:

       Jasmin, Nicky, Angela, Kim

B Listen and make notes. Use your notes to complete these sentences.

1 Jasmin's wearing ......
2 Nicky ......
3 Angela ......
4 Kim ......

3 Speaking

Work with a partner. Describe someone in the class. Your partner must guess the name of the person. Begin: *This person's wearing ...*

4 🔊 Listening and Reading

Listen to this interview with Jacquie and then choose the correct summary.

A Jacquie has got a shop in Milan. She goes to fashion shows two or three times a year. She likes clothes for young people and she buys a lot of clothes from Italy and Germany. At the show she likes the women's clothes but she doesn't like the men's clothes.

B Jacquie is in Milan because she wants to buy some clothes for young people. She sometimes buys clothes from Germany, Spain and England. At the show she doesn't like the women's clothes but she likes the men's clothes.

C Jacquie has got a shop in Dublin. She is at a fashion show in Milan. She buys clothes from Italy, Germany, Spain and England. At the show she doesn't like the men's clothes but she likes the women's clothes.

Ramon Blanco – Young Designer of the Year

1 Reading

A Read this magazine article.

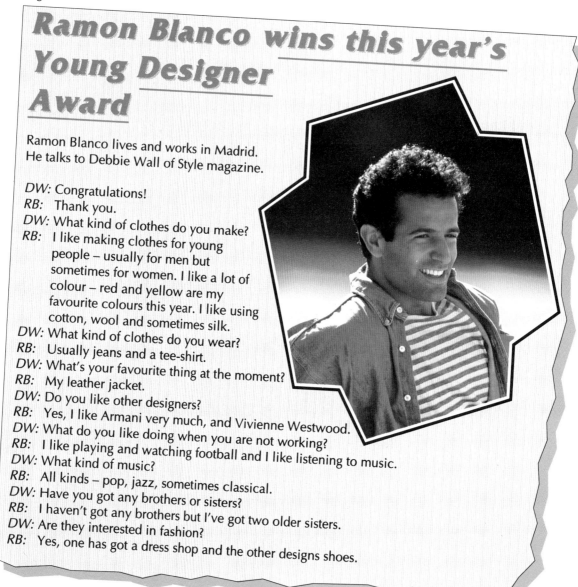

Ramon Blanco wins this year's Young Designer Award

Ramon Blanco lives and works in Madrid. He talks to Debbie Wall of Style magazine.

DW: Congratulations!
RB: Thank you.
DW: What kind of clothes do you make?
RB: I like making clothes for young people – usually for men but sometimes for women. I like a lot of colour – red and yellow are my favourite colours this year. I like using cotton, wool and sometimes silk.
DW: What kind of clothes do you wear?
RB: Usually jeans and a tee-shirt.
DW: What's your favourite thing at the moment?
RB: My leather jacket.
DW: Do you like other designers?
RB: Yes, I like Armani very much, and Vivienne Westwood.
DW: What do you like doing when you are not working?
RB: I like playing and watching football and I like listening to music.
DW: What kind of music?
RB: All kinds – pop, jazz, sometimes classical.
DW: Have you got any brothers or sisters?
RB: I haven't got any brothers but I've got two older sisters.
DW: Are they interested in fashion?
RB: Yes, one has got a dress shop and the other designs shoes.

B Now close your book and answer your teacher's questions.

2 ▭ Language Practice and Listening (C1.4)

Write *this*, *that*, *these* or *those* in the spaces.

Mum: .... jacket's nice.
Tom: Oh mum – it's horrible!
Mum: And I like .... trousers.
Tom: Ugh! I like .... shoes. Can I have some new shoes?
Mum: No, you can't – do you like .... shirt?
Tom: Oh, it's awful!
Mum: Oh Tom, do you like *any* of the clothes ... ?
Tom: Yes, I like .... sweater.
Mum: Oh Tom!

Now listen to the answers.

3 Vocabulary (C3.1)

Match the labels to the clothes.

LARGE

▲ DRY CLEAN ONLY ▲

HAND WASH ONLY

MEDIUM

MADE IN USA

100% WOOL

SMALL

In pairs, ask and answer questions about size.

'What size sweater do you take?'

'Small.'

'What size shoes do you take?'

'Size 5 or 5½.'

4 Language Practice (C1.3)

Put these words into three groups:

a *countable*
b *uncountable*
c *always plural*

cotton	shorts	sweater	trousers
shirt	wool	tee-shirt	leather
jacket	jeans	skirt	dress
silk	shoes	belt	scarf

5 🔊 Pronunciation

Listen and practise saying these words:

This scarf. This skirt. That shirt.
Those shorts. These shoes.

6 Speaking and Writing (C3.2)

A Work in pairs. Find out about your partner. Student A look at page 130. Student B look at page 132.

B Now write about your partner like this:

Maria likes reading and listening to music. She doesn't like watching television. Her favourite colour is blue. She's got a brother and a sister.

European	36	37	37½	38	38½	39	40	41	42	43	44	45
English	3½	4	4½	5	5½	6	6½	7	8	9	10	11

61

C Language Study

1 GRAMMAR

1.1 *have got*: Short answers

Have you **got** any blue shirts? Yes, I **have**.
Has Jacquie **got** any children? No, she **hasn't**.

1.2 *like + ... ing*

Affirmative

1	2	3	4
I	like	making	clothes for young people.
You	like	helping	your mother.
He	likes	using	cotton.
We	like	going	to Milan.
They	like	watching	television.

Negative

1	2	3	4
I	don't like	playing	football.
She	doesn't like	watching	football.

Question

1	2	3	4	5
Do	you	like	going	to the cinema?
Does	Ramón	like	listening	to music?

Short answers

Yes, I **do**. No, I **don't**.
Yes, he **does**. No, he **doesn't**.

1.3 Nouns: Always Plural

(a pair of)   trousers /ˈtraʊzəz/
             shorts /ʃɔːts/
             jeans /dʒiːnz/
clothes /kləʊðz/

1.4 Demonstrative Adjectives

This jacket's nice.
I like **these** shoes.

That skirt's horrible.
I don't like **those** jeans.

2 VOCABULARY

2.1 Clothes

fashion /ˈfæʃən/
a designer /dəˈzaɪnə/
to design /dəˈzaɪn/

to wear /weə/
to carry (a bag) /ˈkærɪ/

jacket /ˈdʒækɪt/
shirt /ʃɜːt/
skirt /skɜːt/
shoes /ʃuːz/
blouse /blaʊz/
belt /belt/
shorts /ʃɔːts/
tee-shirt /tiː ʃɜːt/
trousers /ˈtraʊzəz/
scarf /skɑːf/
hat /hæt/
sweater /ˈswetə/

2.2 Colours

red /red/
grey /greɪ/
blue /bluː/
green /griːn/
yellow /ˈyeləʊ/
brown /braʊn/
black /blæk/
white /waɪt/
orange /ˈɒrɪndʒ/

2.3 Materials

(These can be nouns or adjectives.)

cotton /ˈkɒtən/
wool /wʊl/
silk /sɪlk/
leather /ˈleðə/

2.4 Hobbies

cooking /ˈkʊkɪŋ/
writing letters /ˈraɪtɪŋ ˈletəz/
listening to music /ˈlɪsnɪŋ tə ˈmjuːzɪk/
swimming /ˈswɪmɪŋ/

3 SITUATIONS

3.1 Talking about clothes size

'I take size 6 or 6½'. (and a half)
'What size do you take?'

3.2 Likes and dislikes

'What **kind of** music/sport/clothes do you like?'
'I like jazz.'
'I like watching football, but I don't like playing football.'
'My favourite clothes are jeans and a tee-shirt.'

3.3 Agreeing and Disagreeing

Andy: I like American football.
Becky: So do I!
Colin: Oh, I don't.

3.4 Possession

Jacquie's got a shop.
I've got a new BMW.
He's got an old Volvo.

3.5 Relations

Ramón's got two sisters.
He's got a wife and two children.
She's got seven brothers.

3.6 Congratulating

'Congratulations!' 'Thank you.'

3.7 Music

classical /ˈklæsɪkəl/
pop /pɒp/
jazz /dʒæz/

3.8 Magazines

a magazine article /ˈɑːtɪkəl/
an interview /ˈɪntəvjuː/

4 LEARNING ENGLISH

to describe:

He's wearing a black leather jacket and a green cotton shirt.

to complete (a sentence): Jasmin's wearing ......*a silk dress*........ .

to choose the correct summary/answer:

a ☐
b ☑
c ☐

A St Petersburg

1 Listening and Reading

A Read and answer these questions.

1 Where does Michael's cousin live?
2 Which country is Penny in now?
3 Why has Penny got Canadian relatives?

Michael and his sister Jennifer are from Canada. He's 22 years old and she's 20. They live in Vancouver.

This is Penny, Jennifer and Michael's cousin. She's English and she lives in London, but she's spending a year in Canada. Her father's Canadian and she's visiting her Canadian relatives.

B Penny, Michael and Jennifer are going on holiday to Florida for two weeks. Listen to Jennifer telling her father about their plans. Then fill in the blanks with *some* of these words:

> drive   fly   arrive   depart
> Orlando   Tampa   St Petersburg
> Vancouver   Saturday   Sunday
> 15.00   21.00
> Continental   Florida   Beach
> five   two   airport

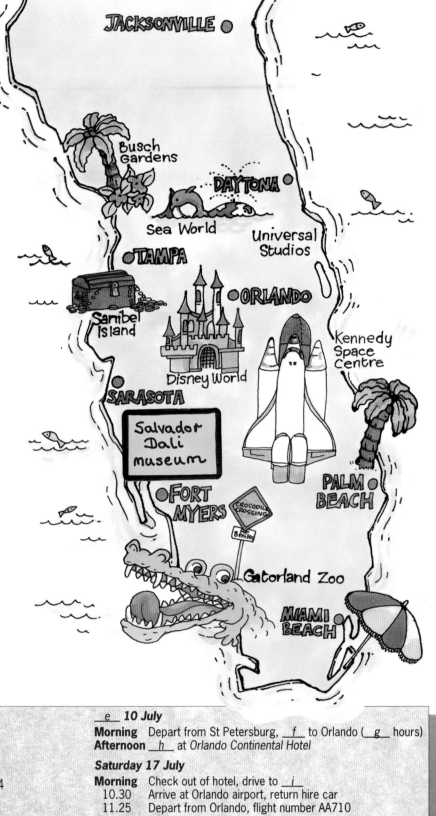

Saturday 3 July
Morning
8.30   Depart from __a__ , flight number AA605
Afternoon
14.25   Arrive at New York airport
15.15   __b__ from New York, flight number AA724
Evening
18.45   Arrive at __c__ airport
Pick up hire car at airport and drive to St Petersburg (one hour).
Arrive at __d__ Garden Hotel

__e__ **10 July**
Morning Depart from St Petersburg, __f__ to Orlando (__g__ hours)
Afternoon __h__ at *Orlando Continental Hotel*

Saturday 17 July
Morning Check out of hotel, drive to __i__
10.30   Arrive at Orlando airport, return hire car
11.25   Depart from Orlando, flight number AA710
Afternoon
14.20   Arrive at New York airport
15.00   Depart from New York, flight number AA673
Night
__j__   Arrive at Vancouver airport

2 Reading and Speaking

A Look at the brochure on this page and answer the questions.

1 Where can you go if you're interested in...?
   a wild birds
   b fish
   c pictures

2 Where can you go if you like...?
   a swimming under water
   b dancing
   c thrilling rides

3 Where can you go...?
   a in the evening
   b all day
   c some of the day

B Work in groups of three. You are on holiday in St Petersburg, Florida. Discuss the brochure and plan your week. You don't want to spend more than $55 each. You have five days but you want to spend some time (one or two days) on the beach. Fill in the diary:

> **Useful language**
>
> 'Let's go to (the Salvador Dali Museum).'
> 'Let's go (scuba-diving/swimming etc.).'
> 'I like/I don't like (dancing/going on rides etc.).'
> 'I want to (see some alligators/birds etc.).'
> 'It's cheap/expensive.'

Monday

Tuesday

Wednesday

Thursday

Friday

3 Language Practice (C1.1)

Write six sentences about your plans for the week. Use the diary in Exercise 2B.

Example: 1 *On Monday we're going to Busch Gardens.*

ST PETERSBURG

SANIBEL ISLAND ANIMAL AND BIRD SANCTUARY

Come and visit Sanibel Island. Watch the wild birds and animals, but be careful of the alligators...

2 hours south of St Petersburg.

$4

Scuba-diving in the Gulf of Mexico

Learn to scuba-dive in the sea at Clearwater Beach, and see the colourful fish.

Leave at 9.00 from St Petersburg.

Price: $30 a day

Admiral Dinner Boat

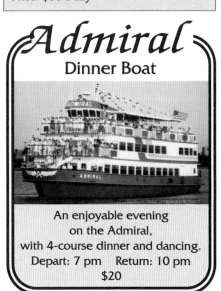

An enjoyable evening on the Admiral, with 4-course dinner and dancing.
Depart: 7 pm   Return: 10 pm
$20

Salvador Dali Museum

St Petersburg

See pictures by the famous Spanish artist Salvador Dali.

Price: $5

BUSCH GARDENS®
TAMPA BAY, FLORIDA

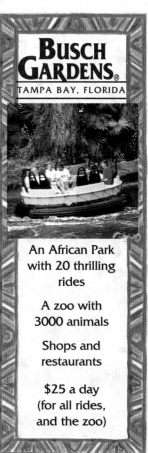

An African Park with 20 thrilling rides

A zoo with 3000 animals

Shops and restaurants

$25 a day (for all rides, and the zoo)

B Orlando

1 Reading

Read the postcard and put these words with the correct day:

| fireworks | rain | swimming | airport | parade | places |
| Disneyworld | films | home | all day | Universal Studios | |

Monday	Tuesday	Wednesday	Thursday	Friday

Monday, 10 July

Here we are in Orlando. The weather is very hot - hotter than in Vancouver! But it rains a lot too - it's raining now.

We go swimming every day in the hotel pool. Tomorrow we're going to Disneyworld - we're arriving early and spending all day and all evening there. We want to see the parade and the fireworks. On Thursday we're visiting Universal Studios. We want to see some of the places from famous films. We're flying back to Vancouver on Friday. See you then!

Love from

Michael, Jennifer and Penny
Orlando, USA

ORLANDO FL538
PM
10 JUL
92

Harvey Cushing MD 45 USA

Mr & Mrs T. Black

1057 12th Avenue

Vancouver

Canada

2 Language Practice (C1.6)

Make true sentences.

Example: **1** *Florida is hotter than Vancouver.*

1 Florida/Vancouver (*hot*)
2 Canada/the United States (*big*)
3 Orlando/London (*cold*)
4 The Salvador Dali Museum/Busch Gardens (*cheap*)
5 Miami/Orlando (*near to St Petersburg*)
6 Jennifer/Michael (*old*)

3 Speaking

Work in pairs. What do you like? What don't you like?
Compare with your partner. Say what you think is *better* or *worse*.

Example: A: *Tennis is better than squash.*
B: *I don't agree. Squash is better than tennis.*

Useful language	'I like both the same.'
	'I don't like tennis or squash.'
	'It depends.'

Which is better?	You	Your partner
tennis or squash?		
coffee or tea?		
bicycles or cars?		
reading or watching television?		
the cinema or the theatre?		
Saturday or Sunday?		
Which is worse?		
homework or housework?		
going to the hairdresser or going to the doctor?		
losing your passport or losing your money?		
a broken arm or a broken leg?		
being thirsty or being tired?		
hot weather or cold weather?		

4 📼 Listening and Vocabulary (C2.1)

Listen and match the weather pictures to six short conversations.

It's cold.

It's warm.

c

It's sunny.

It's windy.

It's raining.

f

It's hot.

5 Writing

You are on holiday in Florida. Look at the diary, and write a postcard to a friend at home, about your plans for the week.

hire car - spend a day on Cocoa Beach - swim - drive to Orlando
Monday

visit Disneyworld - see The Magic Kingdom and Epcot Centre
Tuesday

go to Universal Film Studios
Wednesday

go to Sea World - see whales and dolphins or Gatorland Zoo - 5000 alligators
Thursday

see the Kennedy Space Centre
Friday

fly home
Saturday

C Language Study

1 GRAMMAR

1.1 Present Continuous (future)

Use the Present Continuous for definite future plans
(e.g. holiday plans, plans in a diary, plans for a journey):

I'm leav**ing** on Tuesday.
We're visit**ing** Sanibel on Friday.
He's going scuba-div**ing** tomorrow.

1.2 *want* + *to* + verb

Use *to* + verb after *want*:

I **want to** see Disney World.
She **wants to** visit Florida.

1.3 *go* + *-ing*

Use the verb *go* + the *-ing* part of the verb for some sports etc:

go swimm**ing**   go danc**ing**
go scuba-div**ing**   go fish**ing**

1.4 Verb + preposition

Some English verbs = verb + preposition:

Check in to/out of a hotel.
How will you **get to** St Petersburg from Orlando?
Pick up the hire car at the airport.

1.5 Adjective + preposition

Some adjectives have got a preposition after them:

They're **interested in** birds.

1.6 Comparative adjectives (one syllable)

Add *-er* to the adjective:

8° centigrade is cold, but 1° centigrade is cold**er**.

Spelling:
In one-syllable adjectives with a single, short vowel, double the last consonant and add *-er*:

hot   hot**ter**
wet   wet**ter**
big   big**ger**

In adjectives ending in *-e*, add only *-r*:

nice   nice**r**
fine   fine**r**

Irregular comparative adjectives

good   better
bad   worse

This picture is good, but that one is better.
Very hot weather is bad, but very cold weather is worse.

2 VOCABULARY

2.1 Weather

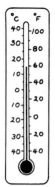

	sunny.	/ˈsʌnɪ/
	hot.	/hɒt/
It's	warm.	/wɔːm/
	cold.	/kəʊld/
	windy.	/ˈwɪndɪ/

It's raining. /ˈreɪnɪŋ/

The temperature is ... (15 degrees centigrade/15°C)

2.2 Holidays

the beach   /biːtʃ/
the coast   /kəʊst/
the sea   /siː/
an island   /ˈaɪlənd/
a park   /pɑːk/
a boat   /bəʊt/

bird-watching   /bɜːd ˈwɒtʃɪŋ/
scuba-diving   /ˈskuːbə ˈdaɪvɪŋ/
dancing   /ˈdɑːnsɪŋ/

a brochure   /ˈbrəʊʃjə/
fireworks   /ˈfaɪəwɜːks/
a parade   /pəˈreɪd/
a ride   /raɪd/
sunglasses   /ˈsʌnɡlɑːsɪz/

to visit   /ˈvɪzɪt/
to spend (time; money) /spend/
to stay (in St Petersburg; a hotel) /steɪ/

2.3 Animals

an alligator   /ˈælɪɡeɪtə/
a dolphin   /ˈdɒlfɪn/
a whale   /weɪl/
a (bird) sanctuary /ˈsæŋktjʊərɪ/
a zoo   /zuː/

2.4 Travel

to arrive /əˈraɪv/   to depart /dɪˈpɑːt/
                        to leave /liːv/   to return /rɪˈtɜːn/

ORLANDO

ORLANDO

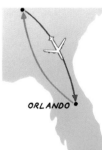

ORLANDO

to hire (a car) /haɪə/
to fly /flaɪ/
the flight /flaɪt/
(it's not) far /fɑ:/
a place /pleɪs/
west /west/
the world /wɜ:ld/
Africa /ˈæfrɪkə/
African /ˈæfrɪkən/
Gulf of Mexico /gʌlf əv ˈmeksɪkəʊ/

2.5 Making plans

to plan /plæn/
a diary /ˈdaɪərɪ/
a week /wi:k/
a year /jɪə/
next (week, year) /nekst/
every (day, week) /ˈevrɪ/
(leave) early /ˈɜ:lɪ/
(see) as much as possible /əz mʌtʃ əz ˈpɒsɪbl/
all the time /ɔ:l ðə taɪm/

2.6 Adjectives

cheap /tʃi:p/
colourful /ˈkʌləfʊl/
enjoyable /ɪnˈdʒɔɪəbl/
famous /ˈfeɪməs/
thrilling /ˈθrɪlɪŋ/

2.7 Adverbs

only /ˈəʊnlɪ/
(to drive) **around** /əˈraʊnd/
(to fly) **back** /bæk/

2.8 Miscellaneous

to sit (verb) /sɪt/
an artist (noun) /ˈɑ:tɪst/
a cousin (noun) /ˈkʌzən/
a relative (noun) /ˈrelətɪv/

3 SITUATIONS

3.1 Talking about opinions

'Which do you think is better/worse?'
'It depends.'
'I think both are the same.'

3.2 Telling the time

It's a quarter to three.

It's ten to four.

It's a quarter past three.

It's twenty past four.

4 LEARNING ENGLISH

to compare
to fill in the ...blanks....

A

A Conference in Kenya

1 ▭Listening and Writing

Listen and fill in this registration card.

- • NAIROBI CONFERENCE CENTRE • • • • • •
- • *Registration Card*
- • Name of Conference: Wildlife of the World
- • Dates: 13 - 16 April
- • Surname: Mr/Ms/Dr/Prof. _____
- • First Name: _____
- • Nationality: _____
- • University or Institution: _____
- • Giving a talk: Yes/No
- • Conference Dinner: Yes/No
- • Room number: _____

2 Language Practice and Speaking (C1.3 and 1.4)

Read the information and answer the questions with a partner.

Name	Room number
Dr Jagge	35
Prof. Bose	36
Mr Fernandez	37
Ms Wabura	38

The person in Room 37 hasn't got a black bag.
The person in the room next to Mr Fernandez had got a small bag.
Mr Fernandez's bag is bigger than Ms Wabura's.
The person in the room next to Prof. Bose hasn't got a small bag.
Prof. Bose's bag and Dr Jagge's bags are the same colour.

Is this mine or yours?

Whose bag is this, and whose is that?

3 Language Practice and Speaking (C1.3 and 1.4)

Student A turn to page 127.
Student B turn to page 131.
Practise the conversations.

Examples: 'Whose bag is this?' 'It's ours.'

'Whose glasses are these?'
'They're his.'

4 ▣ Reading, Listening and Speaking

Read the conference programme. Listen to the conversation between Karin Jagge and Peter Fischer, two people at the conference. When you hear the * answer the questions.

Conference Programme
Wednesday 15 April

Is the tiger in danger?
Salman Bose   2.00 pm   Room 12

Wildlife parks or zoos?
Linda Wabura   2.00 pm   Lecture Room

The animals of the Amazon forest
Karin Jagge   3.00 pm   Room 12

Wildlife in Central Europe
Peter Fischer   3.00 pm   Lecture Room

Optional Visit to the 'Wildlife in Africa' exhibition at the University 4.00-6.00 pm.

Please inform Reception if you want to go.

Conference dinner 7.30 for 8.00 in the dining room.

5 Writing and Language Practice

A Write questions about the conference programme:

1 Where .... ?
2 When .... ?
3 What .... ?

B Change questions with a partner and answer his or her questions.

B Socialising at the Conference

1 ⊟ Listening and Language Practice (C1.1)

A Listen and read.

Frederik Jagge: What are you doing at the moment?

Paulo Balen: I'm working here in Kenya with the Wildlife Trust... and you?

Frederik Jagge: I'm doing research at the university in San Diego for six months.

Paulo Balen: Oh – what's California like?

Frederik Jagge: I think it's great. I'm enjoying it very much.

Paulo Balen: And how's Karin?

Frederik Jagge: She's fine – she's here, actually. She's talking about her work in Brazil tomorrow.

Paulo Balen: Oh, that's good. Is Peter Fischer here?

Frederik Jagge: Yes, he's giving a talk tomorrow on Wildlife in Central Europe.

Paulo Balen: Are you going to it?

Frederik Jagge: No, I'm going to Karin's talk.

Paulo Balen: Oh yes, of course.

Frederik Jagge: Are you going to Peter's talk?

Paulo Balen: Mmm ... perhaps. Which talks are you going to this afternoon?

B Answer the questions ✓ (*yes*) ✗ (*no*) or **?** (*don't know*)

1 Frederik is a visitor in Kenya.
2 Paulo is from Kenya.
3 Frederik is from Norway.
4 San Diego is in California.
5 Karin is working in San Diego.
6 Peter Fischer works in Kenya.

2 Study Skills (C1.1 and Unit 10)

Find examples of the **Present Continuous** in the dialogue and put them in two groups:

1 Talking about the present
2 Talking about the future

3 Language Practice and Speaking (C1.2)

Practise in groups of three.
One of you is the waiter.
Two of you are customers.

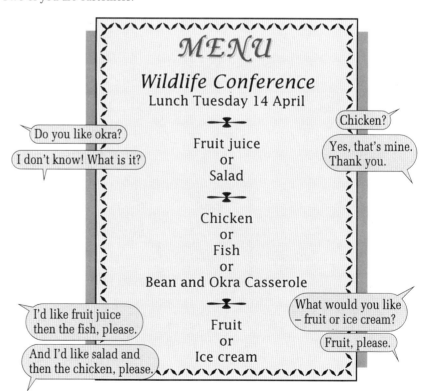

MENU
Wildlife Conference
Lunch Tuesday 14 April

Fruit juice
or
Salad

Chicken
or
Fish
or
Bean and Okra Casserole

Fruit
or
Ice cream

Do you like okra?
I don't know! What is it?

Chicken?
Yes, that's mine. Thank you.

What would you like – fruit or ice cream?
Fruit, please.

I'd like fruit juice then the fish, please.
And I'd like salad and then the chicken, please.

4 ⊟Pronunciation

A Listen and write down the number of words you hear.

> *Example:* *Karin's working in Brazil.*
> 5 words

B Now look at the tapescript on page 137 and listen again. Which word has the most stress? Practise saying the sentences.

5 Speaking

You are at the conference. You meet a colleague in Reception. Student A – you are Terry Daniels – turn to page 125. Student B – you are Sammy Walsh – turn to page 127. Now look at Exercise 1 again. Have a conversation like this:

Terry: Sammy! Hi, how are you?
Sammy: Oh, hello. I'm fine. How are you?
Terry: ......
Sammy: ......   (continue)

6 ⊟Listening

Listen to these conversations. Do the speakers agree (✓) or disagree (✗)?

1 ☐ 2 ☐ 3 ☐
4 ☐ 5 ☐ 6 ☐

7 Speaking and Vocabulary (C3.4 and 3.5)

A In pairs, say what you think.

> *Example:* *American food – delicious or awful?*
> **Student A:** *I think American food is delicious.*
> **Student B:** *So do I.*

1 Italian food – delicious or awful?
2 English – easy or difficult?
3 Politics – interesting or boring?
4 Television in my country – good or bad?
5 Motorbikes – exciting or dangerous?
6 Homework – useful or useless?

B Now give your own opinions about other things. Does your partner agree or disagree with you?

8 ⊟Listening and Vocabulary (C2.1)

Listen to some information about five of these wild animals.
Which animals are the speakers describing? Write the correct answers.

1 ....   3 ....   5 ....
2 ....   4 ....

WILDLIFE OF THE WORLD

C Language Study

1 GRAMMAR

1.1 Present Continuous (temporary situations)

Use the Present Continuous for temporary situations in the present.

What are you doing at the moment?
I'm working in Kenya for six months. I'm enjoying it very much.

1.2 would like

I You He/She We They	would like	fruit juice. some coffee. a cup of tea.	(I'd like...) (You'd like...) (He'd/She'd like...) (We'd like...) (They'd like...)

Questions

Would you **like** a drink?
What **would** you **like** – chicken or fish?

want and *would like*

Use *'I'd like ....'* for making polite requests:
    I'd like an orange juice, please.

You can use *'I want ...'* for talking about plans:
    I want to buy a camera from the Duty Free Shop at the airport.

NB: Use *would like*, not *want*, for making polite requests.

1.3 Possessive pronouns

It's my bag.   It's **mine**.
It's your bag.   It's **yours**.
It's his bag.   It's **his**.
It's her bag.   It's **hers**.
It's our bag.   It's **ours**.
It's their bag.   It's **theirs**.

1.4 *whose* and *which*

'**Whose** (bag) is this?   'It's mine.'
'**Whose** (glasses) are these?' 'They're mine.

'**Which** (talks) are you going to?'
'**Which** (bag) is yours?'

2 VOCABULARY

2.1 Wildlife

a deer /dɪə/

a dog /dɒg/

an elephant /ˈelɪfənt/

a giraffe /dʒɪˈrɑːf/

a horse /hɔːs/

a kangaroo /kæŋgəˈruː/

a lion /ˈlaɪən/

a panda /ˈpændə/

a rabbit /ˈræbɪt/

a tiger /ˈtaɪgə/

2.2 Countries and nationalities

Brazil /brəˈzɪl/   Brazilian /brəˈzɪlɪən/
India /ˈɪndɪə/   Indian /ˈɪndɪən/

California /kælɪˈfɔːnɪə/   Californian /kælɪˈfɔːnɪən/

2.3 A conference

an exhibition /eksɪˈbɪʃən/
a colleague /ˈkɒliːg/
to fill in (a form) /fɪl ɪn/
to give a talk /gɪv ə tɔːk/
to give an opinion /gɪv ən əˈpɪnjən/
a lecture /ˈlektʃə/
to inform /ɪnˈfɔːm/
a registration card /redʒɪsˈtreɪʃən kɑːd/
to do research /duː rɪˈsɜːtʃ/
to socialise /ˈsəʊʃəlaɪz/

2.4 Adjectives

boring /ˈbɔːrɪŋ/
dangerous /ˈdeɪndʒərəs/
easy /ˈiːzɪ/
exciting /ɪkˈsaɪtɪŋ/
great /greɪt/
long /lɒŋ/
tall /tɔːl/
useful /ˈjuːsfəl/
useless /ˈjuːslɪs/
married /ˈmærɪd/

2.5 Miscellaneous

perhaps (adverb) /pəˈhæps/
(in) danger (noun) /ˈdeɪndʒə/

3 SITUATIONS

3.1 In a restaurant

'What would you like?' 'I'd like fruit juice and then the fish, please.'

'Chicken?' 'Yes, that's mine.'

3.2 Saying goodbye

'I must go – see you.'
'See you later.'

3.3 Asking for and giving opinions

'What's....like'?

'I think it's delicious.'
'I think Kenya is great.'

3.4 Agreeing

'Yes, so do I.'
'Yes, I think you're right.'

3.5 Disagreeing

'Yes, but ... '
'Oh, *I* don't.'
'How can you say that?'

3.6 Conversation

'And where are you from, Mrs Jagge?'
'**Actually** it's *Doctor* Jagge.'

'And how's Karin?'
'She's fine – she's here, **actually**.'

A The women's 200 metres final

1 Vocabulary and Speaking

A Work with a partner. Look at the flags **1 – 12**. For each flag, write down the country and the nationality. (Do you want more help? Student A turn to page 126, and Student B turn to page 128.)

Example: **1** *Japan – Japanese*

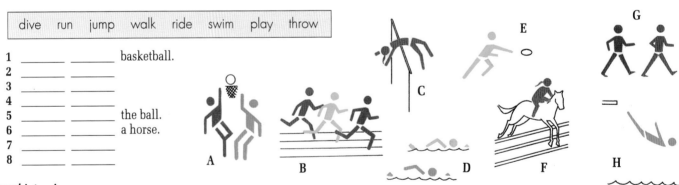

B Match the words to the pictures and use the words to write sentences about each picture.

Example: **1A** *They're playing basketball.*

| dive | run | jump | walk | ride | swim | play | throw |

1 _____ _____ basketball.
2 _____ _____
3 _____ _____
4 _____ _____
5 _____ _____ the ball.
6 _____ _____ a horse.
7 _____ _____
8 _____ _____

2 Listening

A Listen to the commentary on the women's 200 metres final and fill in the information below.

Name	Number	Country	Position at end of race	Medal
Linda Casey				
Betty Diamond			6th	
Monica Gutholf				
Martha Mbene				
Olivia Pizarro			5th	
Jill Washington				

B Listen to the commentary again and answer the questions.

1 What's the time in Tokyo?
2 What date is it?
3 What's the weather like?
4 What's the time in Ireland? (Look at page 19 again.)

3 Language Practice

A Adverbs (C1.3)

Choose the adjective or the adverb in the sentences below.

1 The runners are walking _____ to the starting line.
2 Linda Casey is a very _____ runner.
3 That was a really _____ race.
4 The winner is smiling _____ .
5 Jill Washington is a _____ woman today.
6 She is walking away _____ .

Adjective	Adverb
quick	quickly
strong	strongly
good	well
happy	happily
sad	sadly
slow	slowly

B Verbs (C1.1)

Match the verbs on the left with their past tenses on the right.

Verb	Past tense
say	won
be	did
see	had
come	saw
speak	went
do	said
win	spoke
have	came
go	was/were

4 Reading and language Practice (C1.1)

Read the newspaper article and fill in the gaps with the correct past tense of the verb (affirmative or negative).

'IRISH EYES ARE SMILING!'

6th June

Report by Mary Downes

Linda Casey, the Irish runner, won the final of the women's 200 metres at the Student Games in Tokyo yesterday. After the race Linda spoke to reporters. She said, 'I'm very, very happy. I did a lot of training in Ireland, and I came to Tokyo two weeks ago to run for my country. Now I've got a gold medal. It's wonderful!'

The gold medal winner's boyfriend, Mr Michael

Kilmartin, saw the race on television in Ireland and

was delighted. Linda's parents were also very happy. 'We had a party with the neighbours all night', they said. 'We didn't go to bed at all!'

Martha Mbene from Kenya came second in the race and Monica Gutholf from Norway was third. Jill Washington from the United States was the favourite to win. But she came fourth, so she didn't get a medal.

Affirmative	Negative
1 Linda won ...	*but Jill _____ _____ .*
2 Linda _____ to reporters ...	*but Jill didn't speak to reporters.*
3 Linda came to Tokyo ...	*but her boyfriend _____ _____ .*
4 Linda's boyfriend saw it on TV.	*He _____ _____ it in Tokyo.*
5 Linda's boyfriend _____ happy ...	*Jill's boyfriend wasn't happy.*
6 Jill's parents were sad ...	*but Linda's parents _____ _____ sad.*
7 Linda' parents _____ a party ...	*but Jill's parents didn't have a party.*
8 Jill's parents _____ to bed early ...	*but Linda's parents didn't go to bed at all!*

B Linda Casey in Tokyo

1 Language Practice (C1.1)

A Match the verbs on the left with their past tenses on the right.

Verb	Past tense
go	heard
give	made
write	did
do	went
make	gave
hear	wrote

B Ask the questions.

Examples: 1 *Did Linda Casey <u>win</u>?*

1 Yes, she <u>won</u> the women's 200 metres.
   (Linda Casey/win?)
2 Yes, she did a lot of training in Ireland.
   (Linda / do a lot of training?)
3 No, Mr and Mrs Casey didn't go to Tokyo.
   (Mr and Mrs Casey / go to Tokyo?)
4 Yes, she spoke to reporters after the race.
   (Linda / speak to reporters?)
5 Linda came to Tokyo two weeks ago.
   (When?)
6 She won a gold medal.
   (What?)
7 Michael? Oh, he heard the news in Ireland.
   (Where?)

C Now answer the questions above; this time, use short answers.

2 Listening (C1.1 and 1.2)

Linda is making a phone call from Tokyo. Listen and answer the questions:

1 Who is Linda phoning?
2 What did Linda hear about her parents' party?
3 Where did Linda go to a party?
4 Who made the cake? Who was it for?
5 What did someone give Linda yesterday?
6 Who wrote Linda a letter?
7 Who spoke to Michael on the phone?

3 Speaking and Writing (C1.1 and 3.1)

A Work with a partner. Student A turn to page 130 and student B page 129.

B Now write an article about the runner you interviewed for an English language magazine.

4 Vocabulary

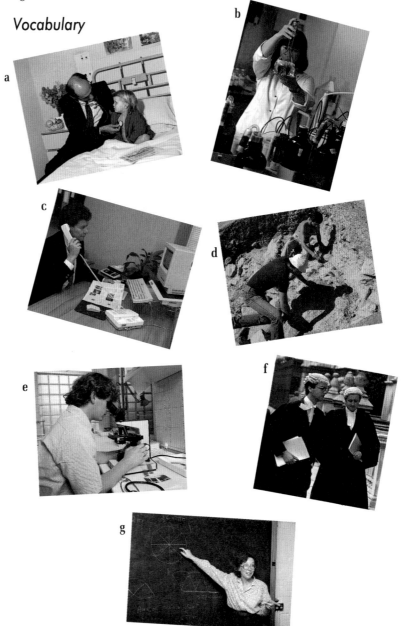

A What subjects did/do these people study? Match the photos with the subjects.

> archaeology   chemistry   law   medicine   biology
> computer science   literature   history   business studies
> education   mathematics

B Are – or were – you a student? Work with a partner, and talk about your subjects at school, college or university.

5 Reading and language Practice (C1.1)

Read Linda's letter, and fill in the gaps with one of the verb forms below.

'm	is	're	it's	there's	was	were
went	saw	had	heard	didn't		

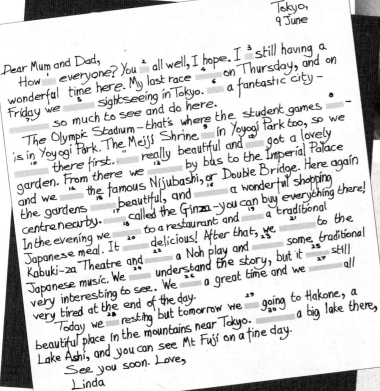

Tokyo,
9 June

Dear Mum and Dad,
How ⟨1⟩ everyone? You ⟨2⟩ all well, I hope. I ⟨3⟩ still having a wonderful time here. My last race ⟨4⟩ on Thursday, and on Friday we ⟨5⟩ sightseeing in Tokyo. ⟨6⟩ a fantastic city – ⟨7⟩ so much to see and do here. ⟨8⟩ The Olympic Stadium – that's where the student games ⟨9⟩ – is in Yoyogi Park. The Meiji Shrine ⟨10⟩ in Yoyogi Park too, so we ⟨11⟩ there first. ⟨12⟩ really beautiful and ⟨13⟩ got a lovely garden. From there we ⟨14⟩ by bus to the Imperial Palace and we ⟨15⟩ the famous Nijubashi, or Double Bridge. Here again the gardens ⟨16⟩ beautiful, and ⟨17⟩ a wonderful shopping centre nearby. ⟨18⟩ called the Ginza – you can buy everything there! In the evening we ⟨20⟩ to a restaurant and ⟨21⟩ a traditional Japanese meal. It ⟨22⟩ delicious! After that, we ⟨23⟩ to the Kabuki-za Theatre and ⟨24⟩ a Noh play and ⟨25⟩ some traditional Japanese music. We ⟨26⟩ understand the story, but it ⟨27⟩ still very interesting to see. We ⟨28⟩ a great time and we ⟨29⟩ all very tired at the end of the day.
Today we ⟨30⟩ resting but tomorrow we ⟨31⟩ going to Hakone, a beautiful place in the mountains near Tokyo. ⟨32⟩ a big lake there, Lake Ashi, and you can see Mt Fuji on a fine day.
See you soon. Love,
Linda

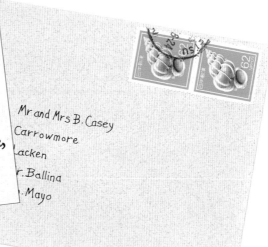

Mr and Mrs B. Casey
Carrowmore
Lacken
r. Ballina
. Mayo

6 Study skills – Vocabulary and Pronunciation (C4.1)

A Look at these words. What do you notice about them? What about their pronunciation and spelling?

Action	Person
to run	a runner
to swim	a swimmer
to ride	a rider

Now make a word for a person from these actions.

Example: dive – diver

1 teach
2 clean
3 shop
4 run
5 write
6 dance
7 drive
8 smoke

B A person from Australia is Austral**ian**. A person from Spain is Span**ish**. What do you call someone from these countries?
Write the words in the correct lists.

America England Kenya Spain Australia Finland Mexico Turkey
Brazil Germany Portugal China Bulgaria Ireland Norway
Morocco Canada Italy Scotland Colombia Japan Senegal

-ian	-an	-ish	-ese
Australian	Kenyan	Spanish	Chinese

C Mark the stress on the words for each country and nationality. Do you notice any patterns? (Does the word stress change? When?)

C Language Study

1 GRAMMAR

1.1 The Simple Past

Use the Simple Past to talk about finished actions at a time in the past. (We know <u>when</u> in the past.)

Irregular verbs

Affirmative

Here are the past tenses of some verbs. (There is a list of irregular verbs on page 121.)

Verb	Past tense
be	I/he/she/it was /wɒz/ you/we/they were /wɜː/
come	came /keɪm/
do	did /dɪd/
give	gave /geɪv/
go	went /went/
have	had /hæd/
hear	heard /hɜːd/
say	said /sed/
speak	spoke /spəʊk/
think	thought /θɔːt/
write	wrote /rəʊt/

(Regular verbs add -ed to make the past tense. See Unit 13.)

Negative

was/were

Put n't (not) after was/were

Jill wasn't (was not) happy.
Her parents weren't (were not) happy.

Other verbs

Use *didn't (did not)*:

My husband didn't (did not) come.
They didn't (did not) go to bed.

Questions and short answers

was/were

Put *was* or *were* first:

Was Linda the winner? Yes, she **was**.
Was Jill the winner? No, she **wasn't**.
Were Martha and Monica in the race? Yes, they **were**.
Were Linda's parents in Tokyo? No, they **weren't**.

Other verbs

Use *did*:

Did Linda go to a party? Yes, she **did**.
Did Martha's children come to Tokyo? No, they **didn't**.

1.2 The verbs *give, write*

The verbs *give* and *write* can have two objects – a direct object and an indirect object:

Subject	Verb	Direct Object	Indirect Object
The queen	gave	a medal	to Linda.
Michael	wrote	a letter	to her.

We can also put the indirect object before the direct object, but then we don't use *to* with the indirect object.

Subject	Verb	Indirect Object	Direct Object
The queen	gave	to Linda	a medal.
Michael	wrote	to her	a letter.

1.3 Adverbs

Adjectives tell you about a noun (a person or a thing):

Adjective	Noun
A happy	man
A slow	car

Adverbs tell you about a **verb** (an action). They often answer the question '*How.... ?*'

Verb	Adverb
The man smiled	happily.
The car went	slowly.

Regular adverbs add -ly to the adjective:

Adjective	Adverb
bad	badly
quick	quickly
strong	strongly
sad	sadly
slow	slowly

Note: adjectives which end in -y, change the -y into -ily: *happy, happily*

Irregular adverbs

Adjective	Adverb
good	well
fast	fast

1.4 Plural Nouns: 's

For **regular plural** nouns, add an apostrophe **after** the plural -s:

Singular	Plural
boy the boy's ball	boys the boys' ball

Irregular plural nouns don't end in -s (e.g. *men*), so add 's:

the men's 200 metres race
the women's 1000 metres race
the children's ball

2 VOCABULARY

2.1 Games and races

basketball /bɑːskətbɑll/
training (for a race) /treɪnɪŋ/
to warm up /wɔːm ʌp/
to line up /laɪn ʌp/
to overtake /əʊvəˈteɪk/
a place (in a race) /pleɪs/
a position (in a race) /pəˈzɪʃən/
a result /rɪˈzʌlt/
a medal /ˈmedəl/
 – bronze /brɒnz/
 – silver /ˈsɪlvə/
 – gold /gəʊld/

the favourite (to win) /ˈfeɪvrɪt/
the final /ˈfaɪnəl/
a metre /ˈmiːtə/
to jump /dʒʌmp/
to throw (a ball) /θrəʊ/
to ride (a horse) /raɪd/

They're off!

2.2 Flags

a circle /ˈsɜːkəl/

the corner /ˈkɔːnə/

a cross /krɒs/

a stripe /straɪp/

a star /stɑː/

a (crescent) moon /ˈkresənt muːn/

the Union Jack /ˈjuːnjən dʒæk/

a horizontal (line) /hɒrɪˈzɒntəl/

a vertical (line) /ˈvɜːtɪkəl/

2.3 Countries and nationalities

Columbia /kəˈlʌmbɪə/   Columbian /kəˈlʌmbɪən/
Indonesia /ɪndəʊˈniːzɪə/   Indonesian /ɪndəʊˈniːzɪən/
Ireland /ˈaɪələnd/   Irish /ˈaɪrɪʃ/
Nicaragua /nɪkəˈrægjʊə/   Nicaraguan /nɪkəˈrægjʊən/
Mexico /ˈmeksɪkəʊ/   Mexican /ˈmeksɪkən/
Japan /dʒəˈpæn/   Japanese /dʒæpəˈniːz/
Senegal /ˈsenəgɑːl/   Senegalese /ˈsenəgəˈliːz/

2.4 Feelings

to feel /fɪəl/ ...   delighted /dɪˈlaɪtəd/
                      overjoyed /əʊvəˈdʒɔɪd/
                      sad /sæd/
                      great! /greɪt/
                      wonderful! /ˈwʌndəfəl/
to celebrate /ˈseləbreɪt/

2.5 Media

a reporter /rɪˈpɔːtə/   a studio /ˈstjuːdɪəʊ/
a news report /rɪˈpɔːt/   a commentary /ˈkɒməntərɪ/

2.6 Subjects

archaeology /ɑːkɪˈɒlədʒɪ/
biology /baɪˈɒlədʒɪ/
business studies /ˈbɪznɪs ˈstʌdɪz/
chemistry /ˈkemɪstrɪ/
computer science /kɒmˈpjuːtə ˈsaɪəns/
education /edʒʊˈkeɪʃən/
history /ˈhɪstərɪ/
law /lɔː/
literature /ˈlɪtərɪtʃə/
mathematics /mæθəˈmætɪks/
medicine /ˈmedsɪn, ˈmedɪsɪn/

2.7 Adverbs

in front /ɪn frʌnt/
together /təˈgeðə/
yesterday /ˈjestədeɪ/

3 SITUATIONS

3.1 Asking for personal information

Are you married?   What do you do?
Have you got any children? What do you study?
How old are you?

4 LEARNING ENGLISH

4.1 Spelling

Many words change their spelling before the ending -er. In one-syllable words, with a short vowel sound before the **final** consonant, double the consonant:

run → ru**nn**er   BUT: read → reader
swim → swi**mm**er   help → helper

In words with several syllables, we only double the consonant when it is in a stressed syllable:

begin → begi**nn**er   BUT: visit → visitor

4.2 Pronunciation

In the words *Italian*, *Turkish* and *Japanese*, the endings -ian, -ish, and -ese are suffixes. Suffixes change the pronunciation of the words:

The suffix -ese always carries the stress:

Japanese, Chinese

The stress always falls on the syllable before the suffix -ian:

Norwegian, Italian

REVISION **2**

A *Places around the world*

1 Reading and Speaking

Tiina Pekkanen is a model. She works at fashion shows and her photograph is in magazines like *Vogue* and *Elle*. Carlos Ramirez is a Formula One racing driver. Tiina is from Finland and Carlos is from Argentina, but they work in many countries around the world. This is what they say about their jobs.

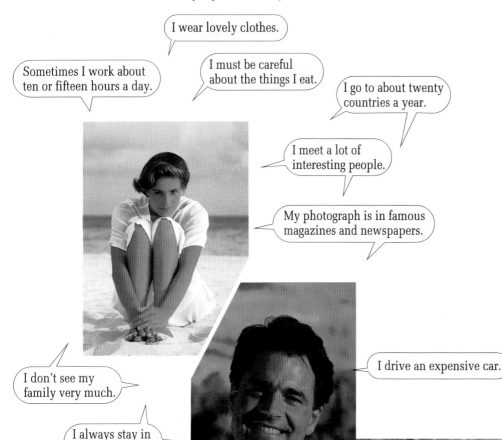

I wear lovely clothes.

I must be careful about the things I eat.

Sometimes I work about ten or fifteen hours a day.

I go to about twenty countries a year.

I meet a lot of interesting people.

My photograph is in famous magazines and newspapers.

I don't see my family very much.

I always stay in excellent hotels.

I'm sometimes very tired.

I can only do this job for about ten or twelve years.

I drive an expensive car.

1 What are the good things about the jobs Tiina and Carlos do?
2 What are the bad things?
3 Can you think of any more good or bad things about their jobs?
4 Do Tiina and Carlos need good English for their jobs?
5 In what other jobs do people travel around the world?
6 Would you like to do these jobs? Why?

2 Writing

Write a short article about Tiina or Carlos. Use the words and expressions in Exercise 1.

First write about what he or she does in the job, then describe the good and the bad things about the job.

Or, write about someone you know who has an interesting job.

3 ▭Listening and Language Practice

Listen to Tiina and Carlos talking about food and drink. Tick the things Tiina eats and drinks and underline the things Carlos eats and drinks.

meat	fish	chicken	fruit	fruit juice
coffee	tea	water	vegetables	
rice	pasta	cakes	chocolate	
pastry	cheese	eggs	ice cream	
alcohol	beans	sausages	walnuts	

1 Why does Tiina say ... ? *'I must be careful about some food.'*
2 Why does Carlos say ... ? *'I always drink a lot before a race.'*
3 Which of the words for food and drink are countable and which are uncountable? Put them in two groups.

4 Language Practice

Write the past tense of the verbs in the spaces in this newspaper article.

A GOOD START FOR YOUNG DRIVER

Carlos Ramirez, the young Argentinian racing driver, **1** *has* a good year in 1992, his first in Formula One. He **2** *come* third in the Grand Prix in Monaco and second in Germany and Italy. Yesterday *Sports Magazine* **3** *give* him the prize for the Young Sportsperson of the Year. Carlos **4** *say*, 'I **5** *have* a good time. I **6** *go* to more than twenty countries; I **7** *see* a lot of interesting places and I **8** *do* a lot of exciting things. There **9** *is* only one bad thing about it – I **10** *not see* my family very much. My father **11** *come* to see the race in Brazil, that's all. But I'm very happy I won the prize – it's a very good start.'

5 Vocabulary

Work with a partner. Write the words for these clothes.

Put the clothes into groups.
Compare your groups with other students in the class.
Are they the same or different?

6 Language Practice and Speaking

Work with a partner. Student A look at the picture on page 125. Student B look at the picture on page 130. Can you find ten things that are different in the two pictures?

7 ⌨Pronunciation

A Listen to this dialogue but don't look at the words. How many words can you hear in each sentence?
Now listen again and underline the stressed words. What do you notice about these words? *are   you   we're   to   the   at   a*

> Are you doing anything tonight?

> Yes, we're going to the cinema.

> What time are you going?

> At about a quarter to seven.

B Work with a partner. Practise saying the dialogue with good pronunciation.
Now look at the pictures and practise the new dialogues.

B Test

1 📼Dictation (20 marks)

Listen three times.

A Listen, but don't write.
B Listen, and write what you hear.
C Listen, and read your writing.

2 Look at this postcard. Sandra and Paul are having a very good holiday. Choose one adjective for each space. (18 marks)

Example: **1** *exciting*

1 cold/famous/exciting
2 delicious/lovely/tired
3 hot/cold/colourful
4 thrilling/cold/thirsty
5 thrilling/horrible/excellent
6 delicious/awful/happy
7 cheap/expensive/delicious
8 cheap/cold/famous
9 enjoyable/delicious/tired

The Lodge, Shimba Hills

Tuesday

We're having a very (**1** _____) time in Kenya. The country is (**2** _____). The weather is very (**3** _____) - about 40°C! We are drinking a lot of cold drinks - we are always (**4** _____). The hotel is (**5** _____) - we have a lovely room. The food in the hotel restaurant is (**6** _____) but it's quite (**7** _____). Restaurants are cheaper in Nairobi.

Tomorrow we're going to Tsavo National Park. It's very (**8** _____) for its lions, elephants and giraffes. We are having a very (**9** _____) holiday!

Love Sandra and Paul

3 Write *make* or *do* in each space. Be careful – write the correct form of the verb. (16 marks)

1 I can't go to the cinema now. I .... a cake.
2 .... your homework. Then you can watch television.
3 I must study tonight because tomorrow I .... a test.
4 In Bulgaria they .... a salad with sheep's cheese, called Shopska Salad.
5 I can't .... this exercise. It's too difficult.
6 She always .... the housework on Saturday mornings.
7 At the moment I .... research in California.
8 I .... that dress for Susanne, for her holiday last year.

4 Write the comparative forms of these adjectives. (10 marks)

hot	old	warm	wet	cold
cheap	good	nice	bad	big

5 Write the past tense of these verbs. (10 marks)

is	go	write	make	come
have	say	do	see	give

6 Here are the answers. What are the questions? (14 marks)

Example: Eight o'clock.
    Question: *What time do you get up?*

1 After dinner? I usually read a story to the children.
2 This evening? I'm going to the cinema.
3 Yes, I like classical music but I don't like jazz.
4 He came to Kenya two weeks ago.
5 Yes, we have – we've got half a kilo of tomatoes.
6 My favourite sport? Football.
7 I'd like fruit juice and then the fish, please.

7 Mark the stress on these words. (12 marks)

chicken	tomato	vegetable
orange	famous	enjoyable
favourite	jacket	music
tracksuit	horrible	colleague

Language study

The Present Continuous: *to be + ...ing*

I You/we/they He/she/it	am are is	.........ing.

Negative

I You/we/they He/she/it	'm not aren't isn't	.........ing.

'Yes/No' questions
Am I
Are you/we/they ....ing?
Is he/she/it

Wh- questions
What **are** you do**ing**?
Where **is** he go**ing**?

Short answers

Yes, I am.	No, I'm not.
Yes, you/we/they are.	No, you/we/they aren't.
Yes, he/she/it is.	No, he/she/it isn't.

Notice the spelling of some verbs:
run → running   write → writing

Use the Present Continuous:

1 for actions that are happening now in the **present**:
I'm studying for a test. So I can't go to the cinema.
2 for temporary situations in the **present**:
She's working in Brazil for six months. (She usually works in Norway.)
3 for definite **future** plans:
We're leaving on Tuesday.

The Simple Past

There is a list of irregular verbs on page 121.

Verbs

have got
I/you/we/they've got (have got) two children.
He/she/it's got (has got) a swimming pool.
Questions
Have you got any brothers or sisters?
Has the hotel got a fax?
Negative
They haven't got any good oranges today.
She hasn't got a new dress.
Short answers
Yes, I/you/we/they have.   No, I/you/we/they haven't.
Yes, he/she/it has.   No, he/she/it hasn't.

Use *have got* when you speak about:
1 Your relations: *I've got three sisters.*
2 Possessions: *He's got a big house, a swimming pool and a Jaguar.*

like
+ object: 'I like apples.' 'So do I.'

+ *ing*: Her husband doesn't like shopping but he likes cooking.

Would + like: 'What would you like ?' 'I'd like the soup, please.'

What's ......like?
'What's Florida like?'
'It's great. It's got lovely beaches, wildlife parks and Disneyland.'

NB: What do you like? → asking about likes and dislikes.
What is it like? → asking for a description.

Verb patterns

Want + to + verb: I want to buy some walnuts.

Let's + verb: Let's have a drink in the garden.

Go + ...ing: Let's go swimming.

Like + ...ing: I like swimming but I don't like scuba-diving.

Countable and Uncountable Nouns

Countable nouns are things you can count: *apples   cars   horses*
Usually they have an *-s* in the plural, but there are some **irregular** countable nouns: *men   women   children   people*
Some countable nouns are always plural:
clothes   shorts   trousers   jeans

Uncountable nouns are things we **don't** count in English. They are singular: *milk   water   bread   cheese   fruit   money*

NB: Perhaps some of these uncountable nouns are countable in your language.

Adjectives and Adverbs

Adjectives describe people, things or places and go with nouns:
Sandy's a **lovely** girl.
I'm reading an **interesting** book.
Disneyland is very **expensive**.

Use comparative adjectives to compare people, things or places:
He's **nicer** than his brother.

Adverbs go with verbs and can describe actions:
He spoke **quickly**.

NB: Many adverbs end in *-ly: happily, sadly, slowly, quickly.*
But some **adjectives** also end in *-ly: lovely, friendly*

Prepositions

Time: **before** (dinner), **after** (school)
Movement: **under, past, through, over**
With verbs to make new verbs: to check **out**, to pick **up**, to get **to**
With adjectives: interested **in**

UNIT 13 FIRST DAY AT SCHOOL

A I remember ...

1 Writing and Reading

A What can you remember about your first day at school? Make notes under these headings:

The journey to school: How did you go? On foot? By bus? By car?
How long did it take? Five minutes? Half an hour?

The school: What was the building like? New? Old? Big? Small?
How many children were there? How many classes?
Was it mixed (girls and boys together)?

The teacher(s): What was he/she like? Young? Old? Short? Tall? Nice? Friendly?

The other children: Did you make a friend?

Feelings: Did you enjoy it? Was it exciting? Was it boring?

B Now read about Claire Winter's first day at school. Make notes on the text under the same headings as in Exercise 1A.

I remember my first day at school. We lived with my grandmother and grandfather, and I remember my grandmother helped me and combed my hair that morning.

I walked to school with my mother, and my friend Anthony came with us. He started school six months before me so he knew everything already! We arrived at the school and my mother stopped. 'You must go in by yourself now,' she said. Suddenly, I felt frightened. I looked for Anthony, but he ran off with some boys. Then a young woman with blonde hair and glasses came up to us and smiled. She knew my name and she said she was my teacher. She took me with her into the school. The building seemed very big and dark, and it smelled of disinfectant. We came to the classroom and the teacher gave me a book with pictures to look at. A tall girl with short, curly hair and blue eyes came and sat next to me. 'Hello,' she said, 'I'm Sally. Who are you?'

Later the teacher told us a story, but I don't remember much more of the day. It wasn't bad. The day ended and my mother was there to take me home. I liked school a lot, in fact. I loved reading and I was quite good at it, and I liked writing, but I hated maths – my answers were always wrong. Sally and I are still friends and our children are friends now too.

C Look back at the notes you made in Exercise 1A. Compare Claire Winter's first day at school with your own. How are they the same? How are they different? Tell your partner.

4 Speaking and Vocabulary (C2.4)

A Work with a partner. Can you remember what you and your best friend at school were like? Here are some words and phrases you can use:

| tall | short | slim | chubby | dark hair | blonde hair | brown hair |

| curly hair | straight hair | long hair | short hair | plaits | a pony tail |

| a fringe | blue/brown/green eyes | she/he wore glasses |

B Look at the photograph of Claire's class, and work in pairs. Write the names of the children below the photograph. Student A look at page 128 and student B look at page 132.

2 📼 Language Practice and Pronunciation (C1.1)

A Make a list of all the past tense forms in the text under two headings:
Past tenses ending in -ed
Irregular past tenses

B Work with a partner. Write the past tense of the verbs in the sentences. Then listen and repeat, using the correct pronunciation.

1 When she was five years old Claire (live) with her grandparents.
2 She (walk) one and a half kilometers to school every day.
3 When they (arrive) at school, Claire's mother (stop).
4 Her friend, Anthony, (want) to play with boys, not with Claire.
5 Her teacher (smile) and (seem) friendly.
6 Claire (like) reading but she (hate) maths.

3 📼 Listening

Listen to Jenny talking about *her* first day at school and circle the correct answer under each heading.

The journey to school: by bus   on foot
                          by train   by car
The school: big   dark   small
                          old
The teacher: friendly   slim   fat
The other children: older   younger
                          friendly
Feelings: happy   afraid
                          excited   shy

From left to right:

Back row: _____, _____, _____,

Third row: _____, _____, _____, _____,

Second row: _____, _____, _____, _____, _____

Front row: _____, _____, _____,

B New school

1 Vocabulary & Pronunciation (C2.1)

A Look at the books and objects in the photograph, and match them with one of the school subjects in the box.

B Which subjects were you good or bad at? Which subjects did you like the most? Which subjects *didn't* you like? Why?

Geography	History	Geometry
Chemistry	Biology	Drama
Cookery	Art	Music	Technology

C Put the words ending in -*y* into two lists: 3 syllables and 4 syllables.

3 syllables	4 syllables

D Underline the stressed syllable in each word. What do you notice? Now work with a partner and say these words:

photography   trigonometry

geology   archaeology

2 Listening

Listen to the following extracts from four lessons, and say which lessons they come from.

1 _____   3 _____

2 _____   4 _____

3 Reading and Language Practice (C1.1)

Anita is a history teacher. She's got a new job in a comprehensive school in Peterborough. Read the letter she wrote to her friend, and write the correct past tense of the verbs in brackets.

Dear Jan

Today I 1.(start) my job at Weston Comprehensive. It's a very big school and I 2.(do)n't know where to go, so I 3.(wait) a minute and 4.(look) around. Then I 5.(hear) my name. It 6.(be) Linda Collins. Do you remember her? She 7.(live) near us in St. Albans and she 8.(go) to our school. She's an English teacher here. Isn't that amazing? She 9.(come) to the school a year ago.

Anyway, that day 10.(be) very busy. First, the head teacher 11.(speak) to all the new children in the big hall. After that I 12.(have) my first lesson with a first year class. They 13.(be) all new to the school, of course and I 14.(like) that class a lot. I 15.(know) one of the children because he lives in my street and he 16.(help) me with the books at the end of the lesson. When school 17.(end) I 18.(walk) home with Linda. She's got a flat near my house. She 19.(say) she 20.(hate) teaching at first but now she loves it. And I love my new job! See you soon.

Best Wishes Anita

4 Speaking

Work in pairs. Student A look at page 126. Student B look at page 131.

5 Writing

A Think about a day when you were at school. Perhaps it was your first day at school? Or your first day at a new school? Or perhaps it was a day when everything went wrong – or everything went right? Think about that day and write the answers to these questions:

1 What did you see/hear/feel/do?
2 Describe the people and the building.
3 What happened at the beginning?
4 What happened at the end?

B Work in pairs. Tell your partner about your day at school, and answer any questions he/she asks about it, and make notes about the questions and your answers.

C Now look at all your notes from A and B and write the story of your day at school.

C Language Study

1 GRAMMAR

1.1 The Simple Past

Regular Verbs

Regular verbs add -ed:

comb	combed /kəʊmd/
help	helped /helpt/
look	looked /lʊkt/
seem	seemed /si:md/
smell	smelled /smeld/
walk	walked /wɔ:kt/

Regular verbs ending in -e add -d:

arrive	arrived /əraɪvd/
live	lived /lɪvd/
like	liked /laɪkt/
smile	smiled /smaɪld/

Regular verbs with a short vowel and one syllable double the final consonant:

stop	stopped /stɒpt/

Pronunciation

In regular verbs which end in the sounds /t/ or /d/, the -(e)d forms a separate syllable:

end	ended /'endɪd/
hate	hated /'heɪtɪd/
start	started /'stɑ:tɪd/
wait	waited /'weɪtɪd/
want	wanted /'wɒntɪd/

NB: In all other regular verbs the -(e)d ending does NOT add a syllable to the verb (see above).

Questions and Negatives

Use *did/didn't* as with irregular verbs (see page 80):

Did you live in St Albans?
Why did you wait?
I didn't like the school lunch.

New irregular verbs:

know	knew /nju:/
feel	felt /felt/
take	took /tʊk/
give	gave /geɪv/
tell	told /təʊld/
sit (down)	sat (down) /sæt/

2 VOCABULARY

2.1 School subjects

art /ɑ:t/
cookery /'kʊkərɪ/
drama /'drɑ:mə/
geography /dʒɪ'ɒgrəfɪ/
geometry /dʒɪ'ɒmətrɪ/
history /'hɪstərɪ/
languages /'læŋgwɪdʒɪs/
mathematics (maths) /mæθə'mætɪks/
metal work /metəl wɜ:k/
science /'saɪəns/
technology /tek'nɒlədʒɪ/
wood work /wʊd wɜ:k/

2.2 School and other buildings

a flat /flæt/
the ground floor /graʊnd flɔ:/
the first floor /fɜ:st flɔ:/
a corridor /'kɒrɪdɔ:/
a stair /steə/
a hall /hɔ:l/
a gymnasium /dʒɪm'neɪzɪəm/
a playground /'pleɪgraʊnd/
a laboratory /lə'bɒrətrɪ/
a disinfectant /dɪsɪn'fektənt/
an office /'ɒfɪs/
a head teacher /hed 'ti:tʃə/

2.4 Appearance

to comb /kəʊm/

blonde hair /blɒnd/

dark hair /dɑːk/

curly hair /'kɜːlɪ/

straight hair /streɪt/

a pony tail /'pəʊnɪ teɪl/

a plait /plæt/

a fringe /frɪndʒ/

She is ... chubby/fat /'tʃʌbɪ/ /fæt/

slim /slɪm/

short /ʃɔːt/

tall /tɔːl/

he/she wears glasses /'glɑːsɪz/

2.5 Feelings and the mind

to be frightened/afraid /'fraɪtənd/ /ə'freɪd/
to like /laɪk/
to love /lʌv/
to hate /heɪt/
to remember /rɪ'membə/
to smell /smel/

2.6 Verbs

to end /end/
to smile /smaɪl/
to tell (someone, a story) /tel/
to say (something) /seɪ/

2.7 Multi-word verbs

to look for /lʊk fɔː/
to run off /rʌn ɒf/
to come up to (someone) /kʌm ʌp tə/
to look at /lʊk æt/

2.8 Adjectives

wrong /rɒŋ/
busy /'bɪzɪ/
disappointing /dɪsə'pɔɪntɪŋ/
shy /ʃaɪ/

2.9 Adverbs

already /ɔːl'redɪ/
anyway /'enɪweɪ/
by yourself /baɪ jɔː'self/
in fact /ɪn fækt/
suddenly /'sʌdənlɪ/
still /stɪl/

A A wedding in the United Arab Emirates

1   Reading and Speaking

Read this article by Saleh Al-Mazrouei, a man from the United Arab Emirates.

A wedding in my country can be a problem because it is very expensive. The bridegroom must buy his bride a lot of clothes, shoes, a watch and so on. Also he must give her money – between £10,000 and £15,000.

The wedding usually starts on a Wednesday and finishes three days later on a Friday. The bride and bridegroom invite their friends and neighbours to the wedding and everyone wears new clothes. They have delicious meals and they dance. There is one big difference between a wedding in a Western country and a wedding in my country: the men and the women do not mix.

After the wedding the couple stay in the bride's house for seven to ten days. Then they go to another country for a honeymoon. When they come back, they live in their own house.

Work in groups of three. Compare this wedding with a wedding in your country. Find two things that are the same and two things that are different.

2   Vocabulary (C2.1)

Start to fill in this spidergram. Write in these words from the article:
a wedding   a bride   a bridegroom   a honeymoon

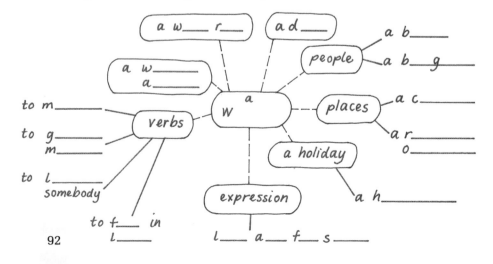

3 ▭ Listening

A Listen to Diane tell this true story. Choose a title for the story:

1 **My friend Ian**

2 THE DAY I MET SARA

3 *Love at first sight.*

B Listen again and put these events in the correct order.

1 Diane and Sara went to the restaurant.
2 Ian introduced Diane and the young man.
3 Diane met Sara.
4 Diane started at university.
5 Diane made friends with Ian.
6 They bought some drinks.
7 Diane and the young man got married.

C Now put these words into the spidergram: *to marry   love at first sight.*

4 Vocabulary and Study Skills (C1.3 and 1.4)

In Britain it is the custom for brides to wear:

Something old
Something new
Something borrowed
Something blue

A Look at the photograph. Can you see something old, something new, something borrowed?

B These words can be confusing. Look at the dictionary entries.

> **to borrow** /ˈbɒrəʊ/ *v.* to have something that belongs to another person and that you are going to give back: *Can I borrow your pen for a minute?*

> **to lend** /lend/ (irreg. **lent**) *v.* to give something to somebody for a time: *I can lend you my bicycle for the morning.*

I can **lend** you something that is mine.
You can **borrow** something that is mine.

Put *borrow* or *lend* in the spaces. Be careful – put the words in the correct tense.

1 You can .... my car, but be careful with it!
2 Can I .... your pen?
   No, I .... you my pencil yesterday and you didn't give it back.
3 Please .... me your book – I need it for my homework.

5 Vocabulary and Speaking (C2.5)

In some countries it is the custom to give special presents for wedding anniversaries. Here are some special anniversaries:

Year	Present
First	things made of paper or plastic
Second	things made of cotton
Third	things made of leather
Fourth	things made of silk
Fifth	things made of wood
Fifteenth	things made of glass
Twenty-fifth	things made of silver
Fiftieth	things made of gold

A Here are some presents. In pairs choose one for each of the special anniversaries.

B Now add *wedding anniversary* to the spidergram.

my mother made my dress - I thought it was really lovely... And she lent me her necklace. The ribbon on my hair belongs to my grandmother. She wore it at her wedding forty years ago! I wore some blue

B A wedding in Hungary

1 ☐Listening and Language Practice (C1.1 and 2.1)

Andrea is getting married to Zoltan next month. She is talking about her wedding. Before
you listen read the questions and guess her answers.

Where are you going to get married?   church/registry office
What are you going to wear?   a white dress/a suit
Are you going to carry anything?   flowers/a bag
What is Zoltan going to wear?   a suit/a dinner jacket
Is Zoltan going to wear a wedding ring?   yes/no
Are you going on a honeymoon?   yes/no
After you are married where are you going to live? with parents/new house

Add these words to the spidergram on page 92:
to get married   a church   a registry office   a wedding ring

2 Writing (C1.1)

Look at the tapescript for Exercise 1 on page 139. Now write about Phil and Lisa's plans.

Brian and Evelyn Stanford
invite you to celebrate the wedding
of their daughter
Lisa
to
Philip
son of Edward and Pat Burns.
The ceremony will be at 6.00 pm on Monday
30 September
in the garden of Littlewood
followed by an evening of dinner and dancing

Or, if you or somebody you know is getting married, write about those plans.

3 Language Practice

Saleh is talking about his plans for the
future. Write the verbs in the correct tense
in the spaces.

> At the moment I .... (study)
> English at a college in Britain.
> In the summer I .... (go)
> back home to see my family. In
> October I .... (go) to
> Stanford University in the USA.
> I .... (do) an MBA – a
> Masters in Business
> Administration.

4 Speaking

You are going on holiday. Choose *a* a place *b* a month *c* transport
d accommodation *e* an activity

a	**Place:**	to Florida	to Italy	to Japan	to Kenya
b	**Month:**	in May	in August	in December	in June
c	**Transport:**	by car	by plane	by bicycle	by train
d	**Accommodation:**	in a hotel	with friends	at a campsite	with family
e	**Activity:**	to swim	to visit places	to ski	to study something

Now ask your friends these questions.
Find someone who is going on the same holiday as you.

Where are you going on holiday?   Where are you going to stay?
When are you going?   What are you going to do?
How are you going to travel?

5 Reading and Speaking (C2.2)

A Work in pairs. Read these advertisements and find some couples.

> **Young woman**, teacher, looking for man aged 30-40, to share trips to the theatre. Must be non-smoker.
> Mailbox No. 2452

> **Unmarried professional man**, 45, wants a friend. Interested in theatre, reading, swimming.
> Mailbox No.2353

> **Friendly, tall, good-looking man**. Likes good food, jazz, and the cinema. Looking for woman 25-40 to share these interests.
> Mailbox No.2372

> **Woman**, 40, likes the theatre, listening to music, books. Wants a friend to share trips.
> Mailbox No.2366

> **Young woman**, likes restaurants, films and fun. Looking for friendly, interesting man.
> Mailbox No.2380

> **Are you 20-30**, pretty and fun? I am 30, tall and good-looking. Would you like to meet me?
> Mailbox No.2367

B Now read this magazine article.

> ### A HAPPY COUPLE
> Dean and Jill met through a newspaper advertisement. Dean put an advertisement in the paper. About ten women wrote to him. He liked Jill's letter and he wrote back to her. For their first date they went to a restaurant. They fell in love and they are getting married in June.

Why are you marrying Jill?

- because she's very pretty.
- because she's got red hair.
- because she's fun.
- because she likes football.
- because she's interested in the theatre.
- because she can repair the car.
- because she's friendly.
- because she's always happy.
- because I love her.

Why are you marrying Dean?

- because he's got a lovely smile.
- because he's kind.
- because he's my best friend.
- because he's funny.
- because he likes children.
- because he's tall and dark.
- because he can cook.
- because he's interested in jazz.
- because I love him.

In pairs talk about these reasons. Are they good reasons to marry someone? Can you think of any more reasons? Add these words to the spidergram on page 92:
to love somebody   to fall in love   a date

6 Pronunciation and Spelling

D**ea**n also likes ice cr**ea**m and sk**ii**ng. /iː/
J**i**ll also likes f**i**lms and l**i**stening to music. /ɪ/

Listen. Who likes these things and places, Dean or Jill?

> beans   chicken   cheese   tea   milk   chips   peas   fish
> eating   meeting people   thinking   sleeping   swimming
> England   Finland   Greece   Italy   Sweden

7 Study Skills and Vocabulary (C1.5)

Look at these words. They are opposite in meaning.

interesting/**un**interesting   married/**un**married

A Use your dictionaries. Can you add *-un* to any of these words?

friendly   tall   kind   old   happy   lucky

B Write the name of someone in the class – or someone famous – in the spaces.

1 .... is very friendly.
2 .... is tall, not short.
3 .... is a kind person.
4 I think .... is an interesting person.
5 .... isn't old.
6 .... is an unmarried man.
7 .... seems very happy today.
8 I think .... is a lucky person.

Work in pairs. Look at your partner's sentences.
Do you agree or disagree with any of them?

C Language Study

1 GRAMMAR

1.1 *going to* + verb

I am You, we, they are He, she is	going to	study.

Use *going to* + verb to talk about plans – things you want to do in the future:
I'm going to wear a white dress.

a We can use *going to* or the Present Continuous for plans that everyone knows about: *We're getting married on Saturday.*
or
We're going to get married on Saturday.
b We use *going to* for plans that you know about (but not everyone):
I'm going to start my own business.
c Usually we use the Present Continuous with the verbs *come, go, arrive*:
They're going on holiday on Saturday.
(NOT: *Next year they're going ~~to go~~ on a trip around the world.*)

Questions
What is he going to wear?

Negative
I'm not going to carry a bag.
He isn't going to study in the UAE.

1.2 Irregular Past Tenses

to meet	met
to say	said
to sit	sat
to see	saw
to write	wrote
to wear	wore

1.3 Verbs with two objects

Some verbs have an indirect object (**1**) and a direct object (**2**):
to lend, to buy, to give.

	1	2
I can lend	you	my pen.
I'm going to buy	him	a present.
I gave	them	a picture.

1.4 Verbs with *back*

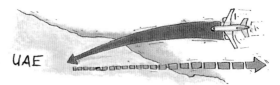

Saleh is **going back** to the UAE to see his family.

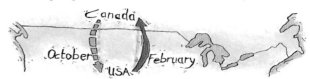

I went to the USA in October and I **came back** in February.

I can lend you the book but you must **give it back** tomorrow.

1.5 Adjectives and Wordbuilding

We can add *-un* to some words to make them negative:

friendly/unfriendly	happy/unhappy
lucky/unlucky	interesting/uninteresting
married/unmarried	kind/unkind

2 VOCABULARY

2.1 Love and marriage

to love (someone) /tə lʌv/
love at first sight /lʌv ət fɜːst saɪt/
to fall in love (with someone) /tə fɔːl ɪn lʌv/
to marry (someone) /tə 'mærɪ/
to get married (to someone) /tə get 'mærɪd/
a wedding /'wedɪŋ/
a bride /braɪd/
a bridegroom /'braɪdgruːm/
a ring /rɪŋ/
a flower (flowers) /'flaʊəz/
a church /tʃɜːtʃ/
a registry office /'redʒɪstrɪ 'ɒfɪs/
a reception /rɪ'sepʃən/
a honeymoon /'hʌnɪmuːn/
an anniversary /æni'vɜːsərɪ/
a date /deɪt/
to make friends /tə meɪk frendz/
a couple /'kʌpl/
a ribbon /'rɪbɒn/

2.2 Describing People

tall /tɔ:l/
short /ʃɔ:t/

lucky /'lʌkɪ/
unlucky /ʌn'lʌkɪ/

dark /dɑ:k/
fair /feə/

pretty /'prɪtɪ/
fun /fʌn/

good-looking /gʊd 'lʊkɪŋ/
funny /'fʌnɪ/

to have a lovely smile /ə 'lʌvlɪ smaɪl/

Notes: 1 We usually use *good-looking*, not *pretty*, to describe boys and men:
Examples: *a pretty house/garden/picture/dress/girl*
but *a good-looking boy/man*

2

> **fun** /fʌn/ (*n. no pl.*) Something you like doing; a good time: *We had fun at the festival. It was fun.* With people – someone good to be with: *He's fun. I always have a good time with him.*

> **funny** /'fʌnɪ/ (*adj.*)
> **1** Making you smile or laugh: *He told me a funny story. It was a funny joke.*
> **2** Strange: *The meat has a funny smell. What's that funny noise?*

2.3 Countries and nationalities

the United Arab Emirates
(UAE) /jʊ'naɪtɪd 'ærəb 'emɪrəts/
Arabian /ə'reɪbɪən/

Hungary /'hʌŋgərɪ/
Hungarian /hʌŋ'geərɪən/

the West /west/
Western /'westən/

2.5 Objects and materials

glasses /'glɑ:sɪz/		**glass** /glɑ:s/
a jewellery box /'dʒu:əlrɪ bɒks/		**wood** /wʊd/
a compact disc /'kɒmpækt dɪsk/		**plastic** /'plæstɪk/
a tablecloth /'teɪbəl klɒθ/		**cotton** /'kɒtən/
a pen /pen/		**gold** /gəʊld/
a scarf /skɑ:f/	made of	**silk** /sɪlk/
a tie /taɪ/		
a candlestick /'kændəlstɪk/		**silver** /'sɪlvə/
a necklace /'nekləs/		
a ring /rɪŋ/		
a diary /'daɪərɪ/		**leather** /'leðə/

2.6 Verbs

to put in /pʊt ɪn/ (an advertisement) /ən æd'vɜ:tɪsmənt/

to belong (to someone) /bɪ'lɒŋ/
to lend /lend/
to borrow /'bɒrəʊ/
to give (something) back /gɪv bæk/
to share (interests) /ʃeə/

I like going to the cinema.

So do I!

to smell /smel/
to laugh /lɑ:f/
to smile /smaɪl/
to feel (funny) /fi:l/

to repair /rɪ'peə/
to ski /ski:/

3 SITUATIONS

3.1 Asking for and giving reasons

'Why are you marrying Jill?'
(I'm marrying Jill) 'Because she's fun.'

3.2 Possession

It's my **own** house.
The house belongs to me. It's mine.

3.3 Conversation

I'm going to study English, Maths **and so on**.

4 LEARNING ENGLISH

an entry (in a dictionary)

the correct order

opposite in meaning

UNIT 15 NEW HOMES

A   Sharing a flat

1 ▭ Listening

A

Lucy and Daniel share a flat together. They want to find a third person to share with them. On Saturday, they put an advertisement in the newspaper, and Joanna telephoned about the room, and arranged to visit the flat. Listen to the conversation at the flat and answer these questions:

1 How many bedrooms are there in the flat?
2 Did Lucy or Daniel offer Joanna anything to eat or drink? If so, what?
3 What happened at the end of the conversation?

B You are Joanna. Write down three questions you want to ask Lucy and Daniel about the flat or the room. Now listen to the second conversation. What questions does Joanna ask? Does she ask your questions? What are the answers?

2   Reading

Read the notice about who does what and when in the flat, and then read the letter Joanna writes to her mother. Fill in the blanks.

Monday / Thursday
Cooking - Lucy
Washing up - Daniel
Feed the cat - Joanna
Joanna's washing day

Tuesday / Friday
Cooking - Daniel
Washing up - Joanna
Feed the cat - Lucy
Lucy's washing day

Wednesday / Saturday
Cooking - Joanna
Washing up - Lucy
Feed the cat - Daniel
Daniel's washing day

Thursday
Rent day!

Friday
Shopping

Saturday
Cleaning: kitchen - Daniel
            bathroom - Lucy
            living room - Joanna

Sunday
Feed the cat - Lucy
Water the plants - Daniel
Put the dustbin out - Joanna

Dear Mum,

Well, I moved into the flat yesterday and I feel at home here already. Daniel and Lucy are very friendly and we take it in turns to do the housework. One of us __1__ a meal every evening for the other two – except on Sunday. We go to a restaurant on Sunday, so we don't have to cook or __2__.

There's a washing machine in the flat and we have two days a week when we can __3__ our clothes. (Usually I only use the washing machine on one of my days because I don't have to do very much washing.) We do the __4__ once a week together because there's a lot to carry and nobody has got a car. We all clean our bedrooms, of course, but we share the __5__ of the kitchen, bathroom and living room. Oh, by the way, we have a __6__ – it's called Tiger.

urst

ford

sham

olk

3 Language Practice (C1.1)

Look at the notice in Exercise 2 again and make sentences about Joanna, Lucy and Daniel:

| can | can't | have to | don't have to |

Example: **1** On Monday Joanna has to feed the cat but she doesn't have to cook or wash up. She can do her washing, but she doesn't have to do it.

1 Monday / Joanna / feed the cat / cook / wash up / do her washing.
2 Someone / feed the cat / every day.
3 Joanna, Lucy and Daniel / the shopping / every day.
4 Daniel / water the plants / on Sunday.
5 Nobody / cook / Sunday.
6 Lucy and Daniel / put the dustbin out.
7 Wednesday / Lucy wash up / cook / feed the cat / do her washing.
8 Joanna, Lucy and Daniel / do the cleaning / every day.
9 Joanna, Lucy and Daniel / pay the rent / once a week.
10 Tuesday / Daniel / cook / wash up / feed the cat / do his washing.

4 🔊 Pronunciation

A Look at C1.1. Now listen and repeat.

1 I **have to** get up early on Monday but I don't **have to** get up early on Sunday.
2 She can't come out tonight because she **has to** work.
3 You don't **have to** shout – I can hear you very well!
4 Joanna, Lucy and Daniel **have to** do the shopping together, because there's a lot to carry.
5 My younger brother **has to** be home by 10 o'clock.

B /v/ or /f/; /z/ or /s/? Work with a partner and say the sentences out loud.

1 We ha**v**e to pay the rent every Thursday.
2 She ha**s** to write to her mother this evening.
3 They ha**v**e a cat called Tiger.
4 Lucy ha**s** got a job in a bank.
5 Joanna, Lucy and Daniel ha**v**e got a nice flat.
6 They don't ha**v**e to cook tonight – it's Sunday.

5 Speaking

Work in pairs. Tell your partner what you have to do/don't have to do every day, once a week, on Mondays, on Saturdays, etc.

B *Flat-warming party*

1 Reading and Speaking

A Read the invitation and write five sentences about the party using *going to*.

> Daniel, Joanna and Lucy
>
> **are having a flat-warming party**
>
> at
>
> 15 Ashworth Flats, Rose Walk,
>
> Haringey, London
>
> on
>
> Saturday, 29th September
>
> **from 8pm**
>
> Wear something red, and bring a bottle!
>
> Lots of food and music. Can you come?
>
> **Please let us know.**
>
> (Telephone . 081-3647223 . . .)

B Work in pairs. Student A look at page 126 and student B look at page 128.

2 ▣ Listening (C1.1)

Joanna, Lucy and Daniel are going to have a flat-warming party and they're going to invite all their friends to come and visit their new home. There are some things they have to do, some things they *don't* have to do, and some things they mustn't do. Listen and write the things down under these three headings:

They have to:	They don't have to:	They mustn't:

> forget to buy decorations   worry about the music
> cook the food   buy the food   borrow some glasses
> buy the drink   play the music too loud   put up the decorations
> clean the flat   pay for the glasses

3 Language Practice (C1.2)

A Work with a partner. Look at the picture and write down five things that are going to happen. Can you think of any more than five?

  A Diana
  B Daniel
  C Joanna
  D Lucy
  E Harry
  F Mary
  G Malcolm
  H Mrs Crossley

B What are Joanna, Daniel and Lucy going to do tomorrow (the day after the party)? Write five sentences using *going to*.

4 Vocabulary

Here you can see six people – they're all doing housework. What are they doing? Put the letters in the right order in the words and match the words.

a GINKOOC
b SHANWIG PU
c SHANWIG THECSLO
d NEANGLIC
e TRAWIGEN SPLANT
f KINGAM HET DEB

C Language Study

1 GRAMMAR

1.1 Have to

Obligation

> We **have to** pay the rent on Thursday.
> Someone **has to** feed the cat every day.

No obligation

> It's Sunday tomorrow – I **don't have to** get up early.
> Daniel **doesn't have to** cook or wash up on Monday.

No obligation and prohibition

Notice the difference in meaning:

> He **mustn't** go (because it's dangerous). (Prohibition)
> He **doesn't have to** go (but he can if he wants to). (No obligation)

1.2 Pronunciation

have to uses the verb *have* (+ *to*), but the pronunciation is different:

> We **have** a cat. /hæv/
> We **have to** go. /hæf tə/
> He **has** blue eyes. /hæz/
> He **has to** leave. /hæs tə/

NB: *to* is pronounced /tə/ in *have to* and *has to*.

1.3 going to

Future (intention)
(See Unit 14 C1.1)

> We're **going to** buy some cheese.

Future (certain)
Use *going to* talk about something you know is **going to** happen, because the start of it is there **now** / it **must** happen:

It's going to rain.

He's going to fall.

She's going to have a baby.

1.4 New Past Tense Forms: *to put/put* :

I put out the dustbin every day. (Present)
I put out the dustbin yesterday. (Past)

2 VOCABULARY

2.1 Flats

to share /ʃeə/

the rent /rent/
heating /'hi:tɪŋ/
electricity /elek'trɪsɪtɪ/
to move in /mu:v ɪn/
to feel at home /fi:l ət həʊm/

2.2 Housework

to wash up /wɒʃ ʌp/
to clean /kli:n/
to do the cleaning /du: ðə 'kli:nɪŋ/
to water the plants /'wɔ:tə ðə plɑ:nts/
to do the washing /du: ðə 'wɒʃɪŋ/
to do the shopping /du: ðə 'ʃɒpɪŋ/
to put out the dustbin /pʊt aʊt ðə 'dʌsbɪn/
to take it in turns /teɪk ɪt ɪn tɜ:nz/

2.3 A party

a flat-warming party /flæt ˈwɔːmɪŋ/
to have fun /hæv fʌn/
'Let us know!' /let ʌs nəʊ/
to invite /ɪnˈvaɪt/
a decoration /dekəˈreɪʃən/
to put up (decorations) /pʊt ʌp/
a candle /ˈkændəl/
a balloon /bəˈluːn/
to bring /brɪŋ/
a tape (music) /teɪp/
to play music /pleɪ ˈmjuːzɪk/

2.4 Verbs and expressions

to forget /fəˈget/
to arrange /əˈreɪndʒ/
to happen /ˈhæpən/
it comes to £10 (= it costs) /kʌmz tə/
to make money /meɪk ˈmʌnɪ/

2.5 Adjectives

extra (= more than usual) /ˈekstrə/
rich /rɪtʃ/
noisy /ˈnɔɪzɪ/
quiet /kwaɪət/

2.6 Adverbs

never /ˈnevə/
exactly /ɪgˈzæktlɪ/
already /ɔːlˈredɪ/
without /wɪˈðaʊt/

He helps me **a bit**. /ə bɪt/
Most people like music. /məʊst/

2.7 Preposition

during /ˈdjʊərɪŋ/

2.8 Conversation

By the way ....

UNIT 16 A NEW COUNTRY

A Immigration

1 Listening and Speaking

Do this quiz in groups of three. Look at the photograph and listen to the questions. Then choose the correct answer.

1 The Liberty Statue/the Statue of Freedom/the Statue of Liberty
2 On Liberty Island in New York Harbour/on Ellis Island in New York Harbour/in the Bay of San Francisco
3 The people of Great Britain/the people of France/the people of Mexico
4 In 1884/In 1934/In 1904
5 450 metres/23 metres/46 metres
6 stone/concrete/metal
7 Two million/20 million/200 000

2 Reading

Now read this information and check your answers to the quiz.

> **'Give me your tired, your poor, the homeless.'**
> These words are written on the Statue of Liberty, which is on Liberty Island at the entrance to New York Harbour. The people of France gave the copper statue to the United States in 1884 as a symbol of freedom for immigrants. For many immigrants the statue was the first thing they saw in their new country. At 46 metres tall, it is one of the largest statues in the world and it is a major tourist attraction. Each year, about two million people from all over the world visit the Island and the Statue of Liberty.

3 Study Skills and Pronunciation

Look at these dictionary definitions.

> **immigrate** /ˈɪmɪgreɪt/ *v.* come from your own country to live in another country: *Many Pakistani people immigrated to my country in the 1970s.* **immigration** /ɪmɪˈgreɪʃən/ *n.* **immigrant** /ˈɪmɪgrənt/ *n.* someone who immigrates.

> **emigrate** /ˈemɪgreɪt/ *v.* to go away from your country to live in another country: *Many people from my country emigrated to America.* **emigration** /emɪˈgreɪʃən/ *n.* **emigrant** /ˈemɪgrənt/ *n.* someone who emigrates.

Fill in the table:

Verb	Noun: Person	Noun: Thing
to	an	....
to	an	....

What do you notice about the spelling and the pronunciation of these words?

4 Reading

Read this information and look at the charts.

People leave their own country and go to live in a new country for many reasons. Sometimes they have to leave because of war or disaster. Often they go for economic reasons – the immigrants want a better job, more land, a bigger house, better education for their children.

   The biggest immigration was from the 1800s to the 1930s. During that time about 60 million people moved to a new country. Most of them came from Europe. More than half emigrated to the United States. Other places included Canada, Argentina, Brazil, Australia, New Zealand and South Africa. Today, because of fast, safe and cheap transport, immigration is easier. Now the largest number of immigrants come from Asia, and more people go to the USA than any other country.

10 largest ethnic groups in the United States

ENGLISH	49,598,035
GERMAN	49,224,146
IRISH	40,165,702
AFRO-AMERICAN	20,964,729
FRENCH	12,892,246
ITALIAN	12,183,692
SCOTTISH	10,048,816
POLISH	8,228,037
MEXICAN	7,692,619
AMERICAN INDIAN	6,715,819

Figures are from 1980 census and include persons who reported at least one specific ancestry group
Source: U.S. Bureau of the Census.

Number of immigrants to the U.S. in a year

MEXICO	95,000
PHILIPPINES	50,700
HAITI	34,800
SOUTH KOREA	34,700
CHINA	28,700
DOMINICAN REPUBLIC	27,200
INDIA	26,300
VIETNAM	25,800
JAMAICA	21,000
CUBA	17,600

Figures are for 1988. Source: U.S. Immigration and Naturalization Service.

Answer True (✓) or False (✗)

1   There are more Chinese immigrants than Indian immigrants in the USA today.
2   The largest ethnic group in the USA is Mexican.
3   Most immigrants to the USA today don't speak English as their first language.
4   Most people emigrate because they want a better life.
5   The largest number of immigrants today come from Europe.

5 Language Practice (C1.1 and 1.2)

In the article it said *'Because of fast, safe and cheap transport, immigration is easier.'* Compare these ways of transport: a bus, a bicycle, a car, a taxi, a boat, a plane.

Example: fast   *A train is faster than a boat, but the fastest way is by plane.*

cheap A bus is . . . . than a taxi but the . . . . way is by . . . .
safe   A . . . . is . . . . than a . . . . but . . . .
easy   . . . .
good   . . . .
bad   . . . .

Compare your answers with a partner. Do you agree?

6 Language Practice and Speaking (C1.1 and 1.2)

What do you know about the USA? Work in groups of three. Write the questions, then answer them. Check your answers on page 125.

Example: What/small/state?
          What is the smallest state in the USA?
          The smallest state is . . . . .

1   What is/large/lake?
2   What are /high/mountains?
3   What is /long/river?
4   What is /tall/building?
5   What is /new/state?
6   What is /big/city?

What about *your* country?

What do you think?

What is /good/ American football team?
Who is /bad/ pop singer you can think of?

The largest hotel in the USA is the *Excalibur Hotel* in Nevada, with 4032 rooms

Sears Tower

B A New Language

1 🔊 Listening and Language Practice (C1.3)

Listen to this person talking about Ben James, an emigrant.
Answer these questions: Where did Ben go? Was he successful?

Now work in pairs. Student A turn to page 126. Student B turn to page 132.

2 Writing and Speaking

Do you know anyone who emigrated to a new country?
Read the following questions and make notes. Then tell a partner about this person.

Name?   A friend or a relative?
When did they go?   Where did they go?   Why?
Were they happy in the new country?   What job did they do?
Did they get married and have children?   Learn a new language?
Did they keep the language or any customs from the old country?
Did they come back to the old country?   Or write to friends and relatives in the old country?

Use your notes to help you when you speak.

3 Reading and Study Skills

Read about these two people. They are both immigrants and they had to learn a new language. What did they do to learn English? Can you think of other ways?

Spiros owns a restaurant in Melbourne, Australia. He immigrated in 1978.

At first I was a waiter in my uncle's restaurant. I had to speak English to the customers. I watched television and I read the newspapers. I looked up words I didn't know in a dictionary. The hardest thing was not speaking Greek – there are a lot of Greek immigrants here. In fact, people say Melbourne is the biggest Greek city in the world, after Athens!

Maria is a social worker in Vancouver, Canada. She immigrated with her parents in 1984.

I was fifteen when we came to Canada. At first the hardest thing was listening – but the people at school were very friendly and after about six months it was easier. I had to study very hard because I wanted to go to university. Every evening I did grammar exercises and I learned lists of vocabulary.

4 🔊 Listening

A Listen to this interview with a woman and write down her personal details.

Name:	*Shaheen Chaudhuri*
Nationality:	
Place of birth:	
Age:	
Marital status:	
Children:	
Occupation:	

B Did Shaheen learn English easily?   Why/why not?
  Did her father learn English easily?   Why/why not?
  And her mother?   Why/why not?

5 Language Practice

Match the beginnings and the ends of these sentences.

Example: *Maria had to go to school in Canada, because she was fifteen when she emigrated with her parents.*

Maria had to go to school in Canada...	because of the war.
Many people had to emigrate from Ireland in the nineteenth century...	because he was a waiter.
My aunt didn't have to learn a new language...	because they didn't have enough to eat.
Maria had to study hard...	because there was no work.
Spiros had to speak English...	because he wanted to start a business.
Shaheen's father had to learn English quickly...	because where she lived everyone spoke Urdu.
Shaheen's mother didn't have to learn English...	because she wanted to go to university.
Ben James had to leave Wales...	because they had to pay the boat fare.
Ben's parents had to save some money...	because she emigrated to Canada from Britain.
In the 1940s many Europeans had to leave their country...	because she was fifteen when she emigrated with her parents.

Write about two things you had to do when you started to learn English, and two things you *didn't* have to do.

6 Reading and Speaking

Look at these ways of learning a language. Fill in the chart.

		I like doing this.	I don't like doing this.	This is useful.	This isn't useful.
1	Listening to my teacher				
2	Listening to cassettes				
3	Doing grammar exercises				
4	Reading newspapers and magazines				
5	Looking up words in a dictionary				
6	Learning lists of vocabulary				
7	Watching television and films				
8	Speaking to a partner				
9	Playing language games				
10	Listening to songs on cassette or the radio				

Compare your chart with a partner. Do you agree or disagree?

C Language Study

1 GRAMMAR

1.1 Comparative adjectives (two syllables/ -y ending)

Spelling change the -y to -i and add -er:

easy	eas**ier**
friendly	friendl**ier**
lucky	luck**ier**
pretty	prett**ier**
busy	bus**ier**

Now immigration is **easier** than in the nineteenth century.
Do you think Americans are **friendlier** than Australians?
Ben was **luckier** than his brother.
She's **prettier** than her sister.
O'Hare Airport in Chicago is **busier** than Heathrow.

1.2 Superlative adjectives (one syllable/ -y ending)

the + adjective + *-est*:

large	**the** larg**est**
big	**the** bigg**est**
fast	**the** fast**est**
friendly	**the** friendl**iest**
happy	**the** happ**iest**

The largest number of immigrants come from Asia.
The biggest immigration was from 1800 to 1930.
The fastest way to travel is by plane.
Americans are **the friendliest** people in the world.
Today is **the happiest** day of my life!

Irregular comparative and superlative adjectives:

good	better	the best
bad	worse	the worst

Which is **the best** way to travel?
This is **the worst** football team in the world!

1.3 *had to*

	had to	**verb**	
I You He She We they	**had to**	leave learn have	because of the war. English in the USA. a visa.

Negative

| I/you/he/she/we/they | didn't have to speak English in Argentina.

Question

Did | I/you/he/she/we/they | have to have an immigrant's visa?

1.4 Irregular verbs

to buy	bought /bɔ:t/
to get	got (married) /gɒt/
to read	read /red/

1.5 *enough*

We can use *enough* with a noun or as a pronoun.
They saved **enough** (money) for the fare.
They didn't have **enough** (food) to eat.

2 VOCABULARY

2.1 Migration

an emigrant – to emigrate – emigration
an immigrant – to immigrate – immigration

a citizen /ˈsɪtɪzən/
an ethnic group /ˈeθnɪk gruːp/
freedom /ˈfriːdəm/
to be homeless /ˈhəʊmləs/

2.2 Continents, countries and nationalities

Continent
Asia /ˈeɪʃɪə/
Europe /ˈjuːrəp/

Asian /ˈeɪʃɪən/
European /juːrəˈpɪən/

Country	**Nationality**
Cuba /ˈkjuːbə/	Cuban /ˈkjuːbən/
Haiti /heɪtɪ/	Haitian /ˈheɪʃən/
Korea /kəˈrɪə/	Korean /kəˈrɪən/
New Zealand /njuː ˈziːlənd/	from New Zealand
Pakistan /pækɪˈstæn/	Pakistani /pækɪˈstænɪ/
Patagonia /pætəˈgəʊnɪə/	Patagonian /pætəˈgəʊnɪən/
Philippines /ˈfɪlɪpiːnz/	Philippino /fɪlɪˈpiːnəʊ/
Poland /ˈpəʊlənd/	Polish /ˈpəʊlɪʃ/
South Africa /saʊθ ˈæfrɪkə/	South African /saʊθ ˈæfrɪkən/
Vietnam /vɪətˈnæm/	Vietnamese /vɪətnəˈmiːz/
Wales /weɪlz/	Welsh /welʃ/

2.3 A Life

to be born /bɔ:n/
to die /daɪ/
to change /tʃeɪndʒ/
to move /mu:v/
to own /əʊn/
to save (money) /seɪv/
personal details /ˈpɜ:sənəl ˈdi:teɪlz/
place of birth /pleɪs əv bɜ:θ/
marital status /ˈmærɪtəl ˈsteɪtəs/
a war /wɔ:/
a disaster /dɪˈzɑ:stə/

2.4 People

a great uncle /greɪt ˈʌŋkl/
a boyfriend /ˈbɔɪfrend/
a farmer /ˈfɑ:mə/
a pop singer /pɒp ˈsɪŋer/
a social worker /ˈsəʊʃəl ˈwɜ:kə/
a (football) team /ti:m/

2.5 Places

land /lænd/
a state /steɪt/
a lake /leɪk/
a mountain /ˈmaʊntən/
a farm /fɑ:m/
a tourist attraction /ˈtʊərɪst æˈtrækʃən/

2.6 Materials

(a) concrete (building) /ˈkɒŋkri:t/
(a) copper (candlestick) /ˈkɒpə/
(a) metal (box) /ˈmetəl/
(a) stone (statue) /stəʊn/

2.7 Money

the (boat) fare /feə/
an economic reason /ɪkəˈnɒmɪk/

2.8 Adjectives

angry /ˈæŋgrɪ/
hard /hɑ:d/
poor /pʊə/
safe /seɪf/
strange /streɪndʒ/
successful /səkˈsesfəl/

2.9 Adverb

easily /ˈi:zɪlɪ/

3 SITUATIONS

3.1 Comparing

I think English is **easier than** Japanese.
He is **friendlier than** his sister.

3.2 Talking about opinions

This is **the worst** restaurant in New York!
This is **the best** place in the world!

4 LEARNING ENGLISH

Do this quiz.
Check your answers.
What is the difference between *this* and *that*?
Look at the charts/dictionary definition.
Play language games.
Listen to English songs/cassettes.
Make lists of ...
Say words the English way.
Do grammar exercises.

UNIT 17 FROM RAGS TO RICHES

A Winning the lottery

1 Reading

Read the newspaper article and answer the question:
How do you think Mr Blackwood's life is going to change?
Write down some ideas and compare in small groups.

■ **DUSTMAN WINS £500,000** ■

Mr Fred Blackwood, a dustman, always watches the lottery draw on television on Saturday nights. Last Saturday his dream came true. The winning ticket was his! And he is £500,000 richer now. Mr Blackwood lives in a small flat in north-east London and his wife is a cleaner at Whipps Cross Hospital. 'There are going to be some changes in my life now!' said Mr Blackwood.

2 Listening (C1.1)

A Fred Blackwood won a lot of money in the lottery. Now, a year later, Richard Croft is interviewing him for a radio programme. Look back at your answers in Exercise 1.
Were they right?

B Listen to the interview again and fill in the gaps.

Fred then...	Fred now...
He got up ¹............	He gets up when he ².......... to.
His job was ³..........	His life is more interesting.
He went to Southend for his ⁴............	He ⁵.......... abroad and he's learning Spanish.
He lived in a small ⁶............ in the city.	He lives in a big ⁷.......... in the ⁸............
He paid ⁹.......... for the house.	He owns the house.
His wife ¹⁰.......... for other people.	Someone ¹¹.......... their house for them.
He used to do ¹².......... work.	He has two or three ¹³.......... a day.

C Now make sentences about Fred using *used to...but now.*

*Example: Fred **used to** get up early, **but now** he gets up when he wants to.*

3 Language Practice (C1.1)

A Now write sentences about Alice, using 'used to ... but now'.

THEN   NOW   THEN   NOW

B Write six sentences comparing Fred and Alice's life a year ago with their life now, using these adjectives. ***Example:*** *They eat more delicious meals in restaurants now.*

delicious (meals)   expensive (clothes)   exciting (car)
interesting (holidays) comfortable (house)   enjoyable (life)

4 Speaking

Work with a partner. Talk about these questions:

I think Japanese is the most difficult language to learn.

Japanese is difficult, but I think Arabic is more difficult than Japanese.

1 What's the most difficult language to learn?
2 What's the most exciting film you know?
3 What's the most expensive country for a holiday?
4 What's the most (un)comfortable way to travel?
5 What sport is the most dangerous?
6 What's the most enjoyable way to spend a birthday?

B A Famous Star

... COMING SOON ....

The Darkest Night

The most exciting film of the year!
The most dangerous game of all!
Every woman's most horrible nightmare!

Starring CARRIE MASON and OLIVER LAWRENCE
DON'T MISS IT!

1 Reading

Read this interview with Carrie Mason, the new Hollywood film star. Write down four things Carrie used to do before she was famous that she can't do now.

Norman Berry:	Now, Carrie, your life changed suddenly, didn't it, after you appeared in *The Darkest Night*. That's the film that made you famous, isn't it?
Carrie Mason:	Yes it is – although this is my tenth year in films. But that's the one that made me famous, yes.
Norman Berry:	And do you find your life is very different now that you're famous?
Carrie Mason:	Well, I'm a lot richer, I guess! I used to work as a waitress in the evenings to get some extra money but now I've got all the money I need...
Norman Berry:	Is everything wonderful now that you're famous, or are there things you regret?
Carrie Mason:	Well, being famous isn't always wonderful, you know. You lose a lot of freedom. I used to go for long walks in the park, but now I can't do that. There are always photographers around or people who want my signature – I just can't go out like that any more. I used to go shopping – I liked shopping – but now someone does my shopping for me.
Norman Berry:	You live in Hollywood, don't you, Carrie?
Carrie Mason:	Yeah. I bought a house there three months ago. It's a lovely house, but I miss New York. That's where I used to live. That's where all my family live. I don't see them much any more. We used to spend every Sunday together, but I don't go back to new York very often now because I'm working and living in Hollywood.
Norman Berry:	You seem to find life less enjoyable as a star.
Carrie Mason:	Well, not really. I've got a nice house in Hollywood and some good friends there. And the work is much more interesting now. Before, I used to do a lot of advertisements for TV, but now I can choose the best films! But it's not *all* wonderful, that's all I want to say ...
Interview by Norman Berry	

2 Language Practice and Pronunciation

Work with a partner. Take it in turns to make sentences about Carrie using *used to* /juːstə/ ... *but now* /bət naʊ/. Can you think of any more differences in her life?

THEN

NOW

3 Speaking

A Think about your life now, and ten years ago. Write down five things you used to do ten years ago that you *don't* do now.

B Now work in pairs. Tell your partner what you used to do. Ask questions about what they say: *Did you use to ...?; What did you use to ...?; Where did you use to ...? Why/not/now?*

Example:
Ten years ago I used to play tennis every week.
Where did you use to play?
At a tennis club.
Did you use to enjoy it?
Yes, I did.
Why don't you play tennis now?
I'm too busy ... I haven't got time!

4 ☐ Language Practice and Vocabulary (C1.3)

A Work in groups of four. Ask and answer questions, using the table, with the superlative form of the adjectives in column 2.

Listen to the example.

A *What's the **most delicious** food in the world?*
B *Mm ... I think pizza is the **most delicious** food.*
C *What about caviar?*
D *That's the **most expensive** food in the world.*
B *Okay ... my turn. Who's **the friendliest** person in your street?*
C *Er ... Well, there's Carmelita at number 56 ... she's very friendly, she has lots of parties. What about in your street?*
D *I don't live in a street ... I live in the country.*
A *Who's **the friendliest** person in your family then?*
D *Oh ... er ... that's probably my oldest brother ... he's got lots of friends.*

1	2	3	4	5
The	(busy) (famous) (dangerous) (delicious) (colourful) (difficult) (fast) (big) (tall) (good) (awful) (nice) (comfortable) (expensive) (useful) (interesting) (exciting) (beautiful) (friendly) (happy) (enjoyable) (boring)	airport family animal food bird occupation car city person singer vegetable fruit hotel restaurant machine book music picture neighbour man programme sport	in Europe in Africa in my country in the world in the class I know in my town in my home today in my street on TV	is ... .

B Write at least ten sentences using the table above, with the superlative form of the adjectives in column 2, and giving your own opinion in column 5:

Examples: The **busiest** city in the world is ...
The **most famous** person I know is ...

5 Writing

A Can you remember the most interesting day of your life? Or perhaps the most awful, or the most enjoyable day? Choose any of these adjectives and think about this day:

> busy thrilling happy nice
> difficult boring horrible
> good dangerous enjoyable
> amazing exciting

Now work with a partner and ask and answer these and other questions about that day:

Where were you on the day?
What did you do?
What did you see/hear/feel?
What happened?
How did it end?

B

> Would you like to see YOUR story in ™METROPOLITAN magazine?
>
> AND win £1000?
>
> Write and tell us about the most interesting – or awful – day in your life.

Use your notes to write a story for the magazine competition.

C Language Study

1 GRAMMAR

1.1 *used to*

We use *used to* to talk about something we did regularly in the past (but we don't do it now):

When I was a student I used to go to bed at two o'clock in the morning, but now I go to bed earlier because I have to get up for work.

Affirmative
Use *used to* + verb:

Ten years ago	I you he she we they	**used to**	do a lot of exercise.

Questions
use *did* + *use to* + verb (NOT: *used to*):

Did you **use to** live in London?
Where **did** you **use to** live?

Negative
Use *didn't* + *use to* + verb:

I **didn't use to** like cheese, but now I eat it every day.

1.2 New past tense forms

Regular verbs

to clean	cleaned
to rent	rented
to travel	travelled
to appear	appeared

Irregular verbs

to pay	paid

1.3 Adjectives: comparative and superlative

Three (and more) syllable adjectives

Use *more* and *most* with all three syllable adjectives:

Silver is more expensive than bronze, but the most expensive metal is gold.

Two syllable adjectives

You know that two syllable adjectives ending in *-y* add *-er* (comparative) and *-est* (superlative).
(See Unit 16, C1.2).

Use *more* and *most* with most other two syllable adjectives:

more famous	**the most** famous
more useful	**the most** useful
more boring	**the most** boring

(NOT: ~~famouser, famousest~~)

2 VOCABULARY

2.1 Competitions

a lottery /ˈlɒtərɪ/
a (lottery) draw /drɔː/

2.2 Occupations

a dustman /ˈdʌsmən/
a cleaner /ˈkliːnə/
a film star /fɪlm stɑː/
a waitress /ˈweɪtrəs/

2.3 Nouns

a dream /driːm/
a nightmare /ˈnaɪtmeə/

in the **country** /ɪn ðə ˈkʌntrɪ/

2.4 Verbs

to appear (e.g. in a film) /əˈpɪə/
to star (in a film) /stɑː/
to believe /bɪˈliːv/
to lose /luːz/
to regret /rɪˈgret/
to miss /mɪs/

to **take it easy** /teɪk ɪt ˈiːzɪ/

2.5 Adjectives

comfortable /ˈkʌmftəbl/
uncomfortable /unˈkʌmftəbl/

dirty /ˈdɜːtɪ/
clean /kliːn/

2.6 Adverbs

abroad /əˈbrɔːd/
alone /əˈləʊn/

REVIEW OF ADJECTIVES

Irregular adjectives

bad	worse	worst
good	better	best
good-looking	better-looking	best-looking

One-syllable adjectives

	Add *-er*	Add *-est*
cheap	cheaper	cheapest
cold	colder	coldest
dark	darker	darkest
hard	harder	hardest
long	longer	longest
near	nearer	nearest
new	newer	newest
old	older	oldest
poor	poorer	poorest
quick	quicker	quickest
rich	richer	richest
short	shorter	shortest
slow	slower	slowest
small	smaller	smallest
strong	stronger	strongest
tall	taller	tallest
warm	warmer	warmest
young	younger	youngest

	Add *-r*	Add *-st*
fine	finer	finest
large	larger	largest
late	later	latest
nice	nicer	nicest
safe	safer	safest
strange	stranger	strangest

Double last consonant

	Add *-er*	Add *-est*
big	bigger	biggest
hot	hotter	hottest
sad	sadder	saddest
slim	slimmer	slimmest
wet	wetter	wettest

Two-syllable adjectives

Change the -y to -i

Ending in *-y*:	Add *-er*	Add *-est*
angry	angrier	angriest
busy	busier	busiest
dirty	dirtier	dirtiest
early	earlier	earliest
easy	easier	easiest
funny	funnier	funniest
happy	happier	happiest
lovely	lovelier	loveliest
lucky	luckier	luckiest
noisy	noisier	noisiest
pretty	prettier	prettiest

	Add *-er*	Add *-est*
quiet	quieter	quietest

	Use *more*	Use *most*
awful	more awful	most awful
boring	more boring	most boring
careful	more careful	most careful
careless	more careless	most careless
famous	more famous	most famous
frightened	more frightened	most frightened
nervous	more nervous	most nervous
thrilling	more thrilling	most thrilling
useful	more useful	most useful
worried	more worried	most worried

Three-syllable adjectives

	Use *more*	Use *most*
colourful	more colourful	most colourful
comfortable	more comfortable	most comfortable
dangerous	more dangerous	most dangerous
delicious	more delicious	most delicious
delighted	more delighted	most delighted
difficult	more difficult	most difficult
economic	more economic	most economic
enjoyable	more enjoyable	most enjoyable
exciting	more exciting	most exciting
expensive	more expensive	most expensive
horrible	more horrible	most horrible
interested	more interested	most interested
interesting	more interesting	most interesting
successful	more successsful	most successful
suitable	more suitable	most suitable

A The interview

1 Reading and Speaking

A Read this advertisement for a job and answer your teacher's questions.

> # EVANS-SMITH PUBLISHERS LᵀᴰD
>
> We sell English language books for secondary school students and adults.
>
> We are looking for a young, enthusiastic, friendly person to work in our office in Barcelona as
>
> ## MARKETING ASSISTANT
>
> Applicants must have a degree and speak English and Spanish – Catalan an advantage.
>
> Please reply with C.V. to:
> Julie Stuart
> Evans-Smith Ltd
> 165 Regent St, London W1R 8JH
> by Wednesday, August 26.

B Find the abbreviations for these words: *Limited   Curriculum Vitae   Street*

2 Language Practice and Speaking

Now read the C.V.s of two people who applied for the job. Their names are Sara Gibson and Ross Gethin. First complete these questions about them using *who, which, where* or *whose*.

1 W........ is older – Sara or Ross?
2 W........ is British?
3 W........ school was in Bristol – Sara's or Ross's?
4 W .... person studied languages at university?
5 W........ did Sara use to work in the holidays?
6 W........ mother is Spanish?
7 W........ has a teaching qualification?
8 W........ person has a qualification in marketing?
9 W........ has experience of working with books?
10 W........ did Ross use to go every year?

In pairs answer the questions. Student A turn to page 128 for the C.V. of Sara Gibson and Student B turn to page 132 for the C.V. of Ross Gethin.

3 Writing and Speaking

Write about why these two people are suitable for the job. Student A turn to page 132 and write about Ross Gethin. Student B turn to page 128 and write about Sara Gibson. Begin:

I think .... is suitable for the job of Marketing Assistant because ...

Show your writing to your partner.

4 📻 Listening and Speaking

A Listen to the first part of the interview with Sara Gibson. Look at her C.V. on page 128. When you hear the * answer the questions.

B Now listen to the first part of the interview with Ross Gethin. Look at his C.V. on page 132. When you hear the * answer the questions.

C Listen to the second part of each interview. Which person do you think is best for the job? Why?

D Now listen to the interviewers discussing the applicants, and fill in the forms. Which person gets the job?

Name: Ross Gethin	Very good	Satisfactory	Not Satisfactory
Appearance:			
Education and qualifications:			
Languages:			
Experience:			
of the country			
of books			
of marketing			
Personality and attitude:			

Name: Sara Gibson	Very good	Satisfactory	Not Satisfactory
Appearance:			
Education and qualifications:			
Languages:			
Experience:			
of the country			
of books			
of marketing			
Personality and attitude:			

5 Language Study (C1.2)

Ross and Sara are waiting for the interview. They find they are the same in many ways. Write the replies to their sentences.

Example: *I'm here for the interview.* ***So am I.***

a I'm really nervous.
b I know Barcelona quite well.
c I like the Catalan people very much.
d I enjoy meeting people.

e I'm not from Spain.
f I speak Spanish.
g I don't know the salary.
h I don't like interviews.

B First day

1 ⊟Listening

Nick is showing Sara her new office. Look at the pictures. Which one is he describing?

A

B

C

2 ⊟Pronunciation

Listen to these sentences.

A How many words does each sentence have?

B In each sentence which word is stressed the most strongly?

1	....	4	....
2	....	5	....
3	....	6	....

3 Language Practice and Speaking

Look at picture **B**. Match the questions and the answers.

1 Which is your desk?
2 Which is your mug?
3 Are these ones yours?
4 Can I use a photocopier?
5 Which is our computer?
6 Can I use these?
7 Is this your mug?
8 Which fax machine can I use?

a The one in the corner.
b The one near the window.
c Yes, they are.
d The red one.
e No, that one's mine.
f The one over there.
g Yes, we use the one in the room next door.
h No, use the ones over there.

In pairs practise asking and answering the questions.

4 Speaking

Sara is trying to make an appointment with Rosa Ayala, a teacher in a language school.

Rosa: Diga ...
Sara: Hello Rosa. This is Sara Gibson from Evans-Smith.
Rosa: Oh hello, Sara.
Sara: I've got some new books to show you.
Rosa: Good. Can you come to the school some time next week?
Sara: Yes. What about Monday morning?
Rosa: No, I'm sorry, I'm teaching. And I'm going to the BET Conference in the afternoon.
Sara: Yes, so am I. What about ....

Finish the conversation. Student A look at page 128 and Student B look at page 132.

5 🎧 Listening and Reading

A Listen to Nick. He's telling Sara about one of the machines in the office. Which one is he talking about?

  a the photocopier
  b the fax machine
  c the printer for the computer

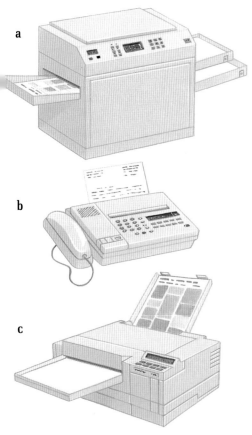

a

b

c

B There is a drinks machine in the office. Here are the instructions, but they are in the wrong order. In pairs write the instructions in the correct order.

> **Take your drink.**
>
> **Open door.**
>
> **Then push button to select drink.**
>
> **Insert money.**
>
> **Wait for your drink to appear.**

6 Speaking and Writing

Nick is telling Sara about his first business meeting in Barcelona. With a partner look at the pictures and write about what happened. Use the words under the pictures. Remember to put the verbs in the past tense. You can start the story:

I started my new job here in July 1992. I had my first appointment at a bookshop at five o'clock in the afternoon. I ...

start   early
four o'clock

look   map
find the way

a lot of people

half past four
traffic jam   worried

stop   ask   said
'Olympics Marathon'

have to phone   explain
make another appointment

C Language Study

1 GRAMMAR

1.1 one

We use *one* in the place of a noun.

Which is your mug? The red **one**.
Which are the new books? The **ones** on the desk.

Notice: We do <u>not</u> usually say *my one(s), his one(s)*.
We say *mine, his* etc.:

I can't find my pen. Can I borrow **yours**? (NOT ~~your one~~.)

1.2 so .. neither ...

We can use *so* + verb + subject when we want to agree to an affirmative statement:

Verb *to be*:	I am nervous. **So am I.**
	I'm teaching this afternoon. **So am I.**
Verb *have*:	I've got a degree in languages. **So have I.**
Modal verb *can*:	I can speak Spanish. **So can I.**
With other verbs, use *do*:	I like books. **So do I.**
	I teach English. **So do I.**

We can use *neither* + verb + subject when we want to agree to a negative statement:

Verb *to be*:	I'm not free today. **Neither am I.**
	I'm not going to the conference. **Neither am I.**
Verb *have*:	I haven't got any children. **Neither have I.**
Modal verb *can*:	I can't drive. **Neither can I.**
With other verbs, use *do*:	I don't know the way to the city centre. **Neither do I.**

1.3 Irregular verbs

find	found
teach	taught

2 VOCABULARY

2.1 A job interview

an advantage /æd'vɑ:ntɪdʒ/
an applicant /'æplikənt/
to apply /ə'plaɪ/
(to make) an appointment /ə'pɔɪntmənt/
appearance /ə'pɪərəns/
personality /pɜ:sə'nælɪtɪ/
attitude /'ætɪtju:d/
to reply /rɪ'plaɪ/

2.2 Work

marketing /'mɑ:kətɪŋ/
a publisher /'pʌblɪʃə/
a salary /'sælərɪ/

2.3 A curriculum vitae (a CV)

qualifications /kwɒlɪfɪ'keɪʃənz/ :

an A-level /eɪ 'levəl/
a degree /dɪ'gri:/
fluent Catalan /'flu:ənt 'kætəlæn/
a (teacher) training course /'treɪnɪŋ kɔ:s/

experience /ɪks'pɪərɪəns/
(to be) suitable (for) /'su:təbl/

2.4 Machines

a drinks machine /drɪŋks mə'ʃi:n/
a photocopier /'fəʊtəʊ'kɒpɪə/
to enlarge /en'lɑ:dʒ/

to reduce /rə'dju:s/

a printer /'prɪntə/

a button /'bʌtən/

to insert /ɪn'sɜ:t/

to press /pres/

2.5 Position

next door /nekst dɔ:/
this way round /ðɪs weɪ raʊnd/

2.6 Adjectives

enthusiastic /enðju:zɪ'æstɪk/
free (not busy) /fri:/
nervous /'nɜ:vəs/
satisfactory /sætɪs'fæktərɪ/
worried /'wʌrɪd/

2.7 Verbs

to explain /ɪks'pleɪn/
to happen /'hæpən/
to try /traɪ/
to wait /weɪt/

2.8 Nouns

an adult /'ædʌlt/
a mug /mʌg/

3 SITUATIONS

3.1 Making an appointment

'Can we meet on Wednesday afternoon?' 'What about Monday morning?'

'Are you free this afternoon?'

'Sorry, I'm going to a conference.'
'No, I'm free tomorrow.'
'No, I'm busy all day.'

'Fine, see you on Friday.' 'Yes, see you then.'

3.2 Conversation

The photocopier? It's quite easy **really**.
Mr Martin? He's quite nice **really**.

I don't know much about books, **especially** English books.
I like working abroad, **especially** in Barcelona.

Good shops, restaurants, beaches, **that sort of thing**.
We sell books, magazines, brochures, **that sort of thing**.

4 LEARNING ENGLISH

Find the abbreviations.
Continue the conversation.

REVIEW OF VERBS – PAST TENSES

Regular	Present	Past	Irregular	Present	Past
add -ed *Examples:*	ask	asked		drive	drove
	finish	finished		eat	ate
	look	looked		feed	fed
	return	returned		feel	felt
	stay	stayed		find	found
	work	worked		fly	flew
				forget	forgot
verbs ending in -d or -t, add -ed (and an extra syllable) *Examples:*	depart	departed		get	got
	end	ended		give	gave
	need	needed		go	went
	start	started		have	had
	visit	visited		hear	heard
	wait	waited		hurt	hurt
				keep	kept
verbs ending in -e, add -d *Examples:*	arrive	arrived		know	knew
	die	died		leave	left
	emigrate	emigrated		lend	lent
	live	lived		lose	lost
	share	shared		make	made
	use	used		meet	met
				pay	paid
double last consonant and add -ed *Examples:*	plan	planned		put	put
	star	starred		read	read
	stop	stopped		ride	rode
	travel	travelled		run	ran
				say	said
change -y to -i, and add -ed *Examples:*	apply	applied		see	saw
	marry	married		sell	sold
	reply	replied		send	sent
	study	studied		shine	shone
	try	tried		sit	sat
	worry	worried		sleep	slept
				speak	spoke
Irregular	Present	Past		spend	spent
	be	was		swim	swam
	begin	began		take	took
	bring	brought		teach	taught
	buy	bought		tell	told
	choose	chose		think	thought
	come	came		wear	wore
	draw	drew		write	wrote
	drink	drank			

REVISION 3

A Royalty

1 Speaking

Look at these two photographs. Write down three things you know about Princess Diana. Now write three questions about her. Work in pairs. Tell your facts and ask your questions. Can your partner answer your questions?

2 Listening and Writing

A Listen to these people's opinions about Princess Diana. Fill in the missing adjectives.

1 (Well, she's very ....)

2 (I think she's got a very .... job.)

3 (She wears .... clothes – she always looks ....)

4 (I think she's a very .... person.)

5 (She's got a .... smile.)

6 (Well, she doesn't have to cook or do the cleaning - I think she's ....)

7 (She is always ....)

8 (I think her life must be very ....)

9 (She's always .... to old people or people in hospital.)

10 (Well, she's not very .... is she?)

11 (She always has to look her best.)

12 (She's a very .... mother.)

B What do you think? Mark each opinion (✓) – I agree or (✗) – I don't agree. In pairs, compare your answers.

3 Pronunciation

Look at the words you wrote in Exercise 2. Mark the stress on the adjectives with two or three syllables. Now listen to the words again and practise saying them.

4 Reading and Writing

Read these personal details and write a short biography. Begin:
The Princess of Wales was born ...

Born: 1 July 1961, Park House, Sandringham

Name: Diana Frances Spencer

Father: Viscount Althorp

Education: age 7-9   Kings House, Sillfield
                9-13   Riddlesworth School
                13   West Heath School
                left at 16 with no qualifications
                16-17   Institut Videmanette, Switzerland

Marriage: Prince Charles, 1981
Children: William (21 June 1982)
                Harry (15 September 1984)

c

d
Charles, Prince of Wales

5 Speaking and Language Practice

A Choose one of these people. In pairs, give your opinions about the man you chose.
Begin: *I think ... / I don't think ...*
You can reply: *So do I. / Neither do I. / Oh, I don't. / No, how can you say that?*

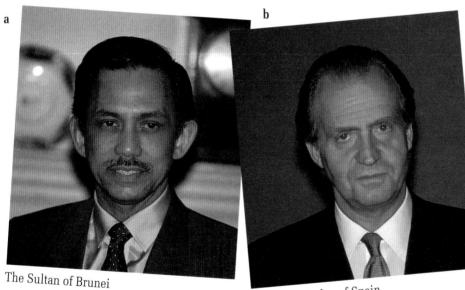

a

b

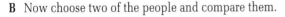
The Sultan of Brunei

King Juan Carlos of Spain

Prince Albert of Monaco

B Now choose two of the people and compare them.

   Example: *I think Prince Albert is better-looking than Prince Charles.*

C Make the questions: Who is (good-looking) man in the world?
                       Who is (rich) person in the world?
                       Who is (famous) woman in the world?
   In pairs ask and answer the questions.

D What are some of the things these rich and famous people *have to* do? What are some
  of the things they *don't have* to do?

E Would you like to be rich and famous? Why? Why not?

e
Emperor Akihito of Japan

B Test

1 🔊 Dictation (30 marks)

Listen three times.

- **A** Listen, but don't write.
- **B** Listen again, and write what you hear.
- **C** Listen, and read your writing.

2 Use the correct past tense form of one of the verbs below to fill in the gaps. (20 marks)

> arrive be (×3) change do give go happen hear
> help know live meet say see take talk wait work

A CHANGE FOR THE WORSE

Terry Waite ¹........ for the Church of England to try and free some American, British and Irish men who ²........ prisoners* in Beirut in Lebanon. Terry ³........ his work ⁴........ dangerous, but he ⁵........ , to Beirut often, and he ⁶........ to free a number of men during those times.

In 1986 he ⁷........ in Beirut as usual. (He ⁸........ n't leave again that year or for the next five years ...) Some men ⁹........ to him, 'We know where the prisoners are. Come and meet us.' So Terry Waite

¹⁰........ the men, but they ¹¹........ him away and he ¹²........ their prisoner for five years. Terry's life ¹³........ completely from one minute to the next. He ¹⁴........ in a very small room with no windows. He ¹⁵........ to nobody and he ¹⁶........ nothing. He ¹⁷........ for a long time but nothing ¹⁸........ . Then, suddenly, in 1991, the men ¹⁹........ him back his freedom. Terry's family ⁻ and people around the world ²⁰........ Terry and his famous smile again. Another change – this time for the better!

* prisoner(s) = a person who is not free

3 Ask the questions that Prince Charles answers. (20 marks)

1 'I was born in 1948.'
2 'I went to school in Scotland and Australia.'
3 'Yes, I did. In fact, I went to two universities – Cambridge and Wales.'
4 'Yes, I am. My wife's name is Diana.'
5 'Yes, I have – two, two sons, William, the oldest, and Harry.'

4 Read the text and fill in the family tree. (30 marks)

Victoria, Grandmother of Europe

Victoria was Queen of Great Britain from 1837 to 1901. She was the only child of George's fourth son, Edward, Duke of Kent, and of Victoria of Saxe-Coburg, sister of Leopold I, king of the Belgians.

Victoria became queen when her uncle, William IV, died. In 1840, when she was eighteen years old, she married her cousin, Albert of Saxe-Coburg, the son of the Duke of Saxe-Coburg Gotha.

Victoria and Albert had nine children. Their eldest child, Victoria, married Frederick, the future emperor of Germany, and their son later became Kaiser William II of Germany.

Queen Victoria's second child and oldest son was Albert Edward, later King Edward VII, who married the Danish princess, Alexandra.

Edward and Alexandra's eldest son, George, later became King George V, the grandfather of Queen Elizabeth II.

Victoria and Albert's third child, Alice, married the Grand Duke of Hesse, and their daughter was the grandmother of Philip Mountbatten, Duke of Edinburgh.

Victoria's fourth child, Alfred, married into the Russian royal family and his daughter became queen of Romania.

The fifth child was Helene and the sixth was Louise.

Arthur was Victoria's seventh child and his daughter became queen of Sweden.

The eighth child was Leopold and the ninth child was Beatrice, mother of the queen of Spain..

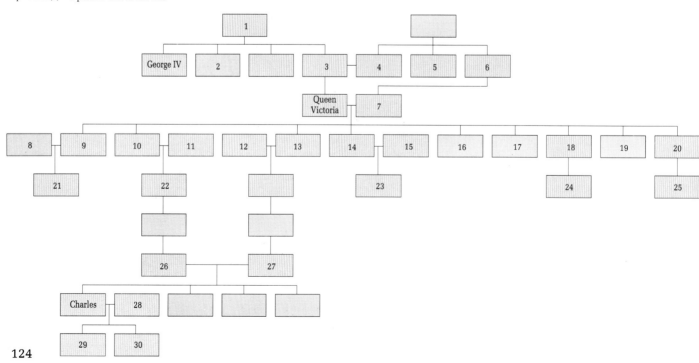

124

COMMUNICATION ACTIVITIES

Unit 1B   Exercise 5

Student A

Ask your partner the questions and write down the answers on the form.

Mr/Mrs/Miss/Ms

Surname: . . . .   First name: . . . .

Nationality: . . . .   Passport number: . . . .

Occupation: . . . .   Car number: . . . .

Address: . . . .   Telephone : . . . .

Unit 2B   Exercise 2

Student A

Look at the photographs, and ask your partner questions, like this: *Excuse me. Where is the Meeting Point?/Excuse me. Where are the toilets?*

Now look at the airport picture. Listen to your partner's questions, and answer, like this: *It's/They're here./It's/They're over there.*

Unit 7B   Exercise 5

Student A

You are washing your car.

Unit 16A   Exercise 6

1 Lake Huron	3 The Mississippi	5 Hawaii
2 The Rockies	4 Sears Building	6 New York

Unit 4A   Exercise 3

Student A

Ask these questions and write the answers:
How much is a ... ?

£. . . . .   £. . . . .

Now answer your partner's questions.

Double room per person per night – with a bath £75
                                    – with a shower £60

Revision Unit 2A   Exercise 6

Student A

Tell your partner about the picture. Talk about what the people are doing.

Example: *There are five people in the gym. One man is ...*

Unit 11B   Exercise 5

Student A

You are Terry Daniels. You are working in Australia at the University of Queensland for a year. You are married to Pat, and you've got two boys, David, and a new baby called Paul.

(Here is some information you know about **Student B** – Sammy Walsh – married to Robin.)

Unit 5A   Exercise 2

Student A

Student B also has a picture. Talk about your picture to your partner. Ten things are different in the two pictures. Can you find them? Practise *There is... / There are ... / Is there ...? / Are there ...?*

Unit 16B   Exercise 1

Student A

Read this part of the text to your partner.

My great uncle Ben, my grandfather's brother, emigrated to Argentina in 1919. He was the youngest son and only twenty. They lived in Wales and at that time there was no work, so many young men emigrated to the United States, Australia and South America. They didn't have much money, but the family saved enough for his boat fare. He was a farmer so he got work on a sheep farm in Patagonia. He worked hard, saved his money and bought his own farm. He met the daughter of another immigrant from Wales and they got married and had children. He had a very good life and was a rich man when he died.

Now listen to your partner and write one preposition in each space.

He never came back _____ Wales, but he wrote _____ his family every week and sent photos. And last year his grandson, Thomas, visited us. It was strange because Thomas speaks Spanish _____ course, but he also speaks Welsh. So many people emigrated _____ Wales and they stayed together _____ Patagonia: they spoke Welsh and kept many _____ the Welsh customs. But one thing changed. Our name is James and _____ Argentina they say it the Spanish way – James – which sounds very funny _____ us.

Unit 12A   Exercise 1

Student A

Here are descriptions of some of the flags. Read them to your partner

Colombia: yellow, blue and red horizontal stripes
France: blue, white and red vertical stripes
Indonesia: red, green and yellow vertical stripes
Ireland: green, white and orange vertical stripes
Nicaragua: blue, white and blue horizontal stripes
United Kingdom (Great Britain & Northern Ireland): the Union Jack (a red cross and a white cross, on blue)

Unit 13B   Exercise 4

Student A

1 Help your partner to fill in the ground floor map of Anita's school.

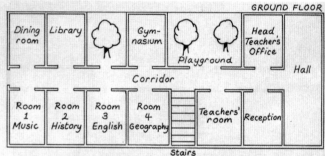

2 Now listen to your partner and fill in the first floor map of Anita's school.

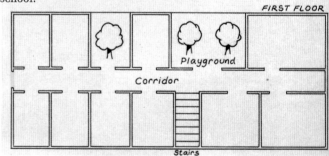

Unit 15B   Exercise 1

Student A

You have got an invitation to the party. Phone Daniel, Joanna or Lucy and say you can go to the party. Then find out the answers to these questions:

You're not sure where Rose Walk is. Ask for directions and write them down.
You're a vegetarian. (You don't eat meat or fish but you eat everything else.) Do you have to bring vegetarian food?
You have a friend staying with you at the moment. Can you bring him/her with you?

Student B starts. When you hear him/her answer the telephone, say your name and ask *'Is that Daniel/Lucy/Joanna?'*

Unit 2B   Exercise 2

Student B

Look at the photographs and ask your partner questions, like this:
Excuse me. Where is the Meeting Point?/Excuse me. Where are the toilets?

Now look at the airport picture. Listen to your partner's questions, and answer, like this: *It's/they're here./It's/they're over there.*

Unit 4A   Exercise 3

Student B

Answer your partner's questions.

Single room per night – with a bath £55
                       – with a shower £45

Now ask these questions:

How much is a...?

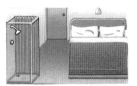 

£ . . . .   £ . . . .

Unit 7B   Exercise 5

Student B

You are watching tennis on TV.

Unit 5B   Exercise 5

Student A

1   Look at your map. Help your partner to find the way to some places on the map.

2   Now you. You want to go to the chemist's, the bank and the hairdresser's. Ask Student B to help you to find the way to these places.

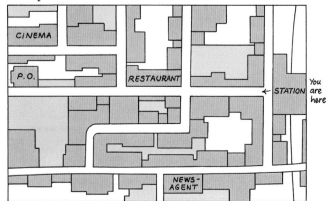

Unit 11A   Exercise 3

Student A

Whose things are these?
Ask your partner and write the answers.

Now answer your partner's questions.

Unit 11B   Exercise 5

Student B

You are Sammy Walsh. You are working for the United Nations in Ghana for two years. You are married to Robin.

(Here is some information you know about **Student A** –
Terry Daniels – married to Pat. They have a son called David.)

Unit 5A   Exercise 2

Student B

Student A also has a picture. Talk about your picture to your partner. Ten things are different in the two pictures. Can you find them? Practise *There is... / There are ... / Is there ... / Are there ...?*

Unit 13A   Exercise 4

Student A

You have the names and descriptions of seven children in the photograph on page 87. Your partner has the names and descriptions of seven other children in the photograph. Take turns to describe the children, and write their names in the correct places under the photograph. The girl *without* a description is Claire. Work with your partner, and write a description of her.

Richard: straight brown hair, blue eyes, blue T-shirt
Simon: blonde hair, white T-shirt
Andrew: dark hair, yellow sweater, red trousers
Kate: chubby, blonde hair, blue eyes, striped T-shirt
James: blonde hair, blue eyes, black T-shirt
Dan: blonde hair, striped sweater
Caroline: straight blonde hair with a fringe, black T-shirt

Unit 12A   Exercise 1

Student B

Here are descriptions of some of the flags. Read them to your partner.

Finland: a blue cross, on white
Germany: black, red and yellow horizontal stripes
Italy: green, white and red vertical stripes
Japan: a red circle on white
Turkey: a white (crescent) moon and a white star, on red
USA: 50 white stars on blue in the corner (top right), and red and white horizontal stripes

Unit 7B   Exercise 5

Student F

You are reading a newspaper.

Unit 15B   Exercise 1

Student B

You are Daniel, Joanna or Lucy. A friend of yours telephones you to talk about the party. Listen and answer any questions he/she asks. Use this information:

The nearest underground station to Rose Walk is Highgate. When you come out of Highgate Station you turn left and take the second turning on the left. Rose Walk is the first turning on the right and Ashworth Flats are on the left.

There are going to be salads to eat at the party without any meat or fish in them. You're going to buy cheese and cook some eggs too. (Does your friend eat cheese and eggs?)

The rooms in the flat are big and there's enough space for lots of people.

You start. Answer the telephone and give your number.

Unit 18A   Exercise 2

Student A

Name: Sara Gibson
Date of Birth: 12th March 1972
Nationality: British
Education and Qualifications:
Manor College, Bristol
'A' levels in French, Spanish and English 1989
Manchester University
Degree in Modern Languages (Spanish and Portuguese) 1993
The Bell School of Languages
Certificate in Teaching English as a Foreign Language 1993
Experience:
For my degree I lived a year in Barcelona for a year where I learn some Catalan. From 1986-89 I worked at the University Library in Bristol in my holidays. From July to September I taught Englis at the Windsor School of English.

Unit 18B   Exercise 4

Student A

You are Sara Gibson. Your partner is Rosa Ayala. Look at your diary. Read your part in the dialogue on page 118 and then continue the conversation. Make suggestions and reply to your partner's suggestions. when you find a time you can meet say: *Fine. See you then. Bye.*

MONDAY a.m teaching
P.M BET conference
TUESDAY a.m teaching
P.M school meeting
WEDNESDAY a.m teaching
THURSDAY a.m teaching
FRIDAY a.m teaching

Unit 5B Exercise 5

Student B

1 You want to go to the newsagent's, a restaurant and the cinema. Ask **Student A** to help you to find the way to these places.

2 Look at your map. Help your partner to find the way to some places on the map.

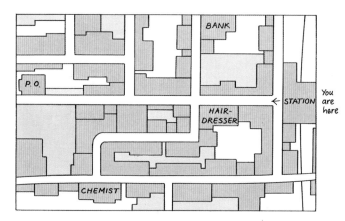

Unit 6A Exercise 5

Student B

Addenbrookes Hospital
Cambridge
10/3/93

Dear George,

How are you? I'm fine. Cambridge is <u>lovely</u> and the job is very . . . . I am in 'Accidents'. Everyone has a bicycle in Cambridge so there are a lot of <u>bicycle</u> . . . .

I'm 'on nights' so I <u>get up</u> at 6 o'clock in the evening, have . . . . at the hospital and <u>go to</u> work at 8. We . . . . at 6 in the morning. In the morning I play squash – there's a very good Sports Centre here – or I <u>read</u>, or . . . . letters.

What about you and your job? You must <u>come</u> to Cambridge one weekend so I . . . . show you the university.

Yours
Joe

Revision Unit 1A Exercise 4

Student B

Listen to your partner's sentences. What is the correct thing to say each time? Choose **a**, **b**, **c**, **d** or **e**.

a 'You're welcome!'
b 'Yes, I'm fine.'
c 'Yes. It's lovely.'
d 'No, that's all, thank you.'
e 'Pleased to meet you.'

Now, read these sentences to **Student A** and listen to the answers. Are they correct?

You	*Your partner*
1 'Excuse me. Can you tell me the way to the museum?'	'Yes of course. Go to the bank and turn left.'
2 'Is this the train for Oxford?'	'Yes, that's right.'
3 'I'm very sorry!'	'That's OK.'
4 'How do you do?'	'How do you do?'
5 'How are you?'	'Fine, thanks.'

Unit 12B Exercise 3

Student B

Interview 1 You are Martha Mbene – the woman who came second in the women's 200 metres final. You are a student of mathematics. You are married with two children – a baby boy of six months and a daughter of four. The children are with their grandmother in Kenya, but your husband came with you to Tokyo and saw you win the silver medal in the 200 metres final. At the end of the race you were very happy because you came second in the race and because your husband was there. You have an interview with a reporter from an international magazine. Listen and answer the questions. Use short answers where possible.

Interview 2 You are a reporter and you work for a radio station. You have an interview with Monica Gutholf, the German runner – she came third in the women's 200 metres final. Ask her these questions and write down notes on her answers:

What do you study at university?
Are you married?
Have you got any brothers and sisters? How old are they?
Did your family see the race?
I heard it's your birthday today. Happy birthday! Can I ask – How old are you?

Now use your notes from **Interview 2**, and write an article about Monica Gutholf.

You are painting your room.

Student E

Unit 7B Exercise 5

Unit 9B   Exercise 6

Student A

Look at the examples and the pictures. Write the questions.

1 *Example:* *Do you like playing football?*

2 *Example:* *What's your favourite food?*

3 *Examples:* *Have you got any cassettes? Have you got a TV?*

Ask your partner the questions.
Now answer your partner's questions and make notes of the answers.

Revision Unit 2A   Exercise 6

Student B

Tell your partner about the picture. Talk about what the people are doing.

Example: *There are five people in the gym. One man is ...*

Unit 8B   Exercise 3

Student B

Answer **Student A**'s questions like this:
A: *Have we got any tomatoes?*
B: *Yes, we have.*
A: *How many tomatoes have we got?*
B: *Half a kilo.*
A: *That's enough. We don't need any tomatoes.*
or *That's not enough. We need some tomatoes.*

Unit 12B   Exercise 3

Student A

Interview 1 You are a reporter for an international magazine. You have an interview with Martha Mbene, the Kenyan runner – she came second in the women's 200 metres final. Ask her these questions and write down notes on her answers:

What do you study at university?
Are you married?
Have you got any children?
How old are they?
Did your husband see the race?
What about the children?
How did you feel at the end of the race?

Interview 2 You are Monica Gutholf – the woman who came third in the women's 200 metres final. You are a student of biology. You aren't married – you live at home with your parents and your sister and brother. Your sister is 16 years old and your brother is 19. Your family didn't come to Tokyo but they saw the race on television. It's your birthday today. You're 21 years old. You have an interview with a reporter from a radio station. Listen and answer the questions. Use short answers where possible.

Now use your notes from **Interview 1** and write an article about Martha Mbene.

Unit 7B   Exercise 5

Student D

You are putting a stamp on a postcard.

Unit 6A   Exercise 5

Student A

Addenbrookes Hospital
Cambridge
10/3/93

Dear George,
How are you? I'm fine. Cambridge is . . . .
and the job is very <u>interesting</u>. I am in
'Accidents'. Everyone has a . . . .
in Cambridge so there are a lot of bicycle
<u>accidents</u>.
I'm 'on nights' so I . . . . at 6 o'clock in
the evening, have <u>breakfast</u> at the hospital and
. . . . work at 8. We <u>finish</u> at 6 in the
morning. In the morning I play squash – there's
a very good Sports Centre here – or I
. . . . , or <u>write</u> letters.
What about you and your job? You must
. . . . to Cambridge one weekend so
I <u>can</u> show you the university.

Yours
Joe

Unit 11A   Exercise 3

Student B

Whose things are these?
Answer your partners questions.

1 2 3 4 5
6 7 8 9 10

Now ask your partner the questions and write down the answers.

Revision Unit 1A   Exercise 4

Student A

Read these sentences to **Student B**, and listen to the answers. Are they correct?

You	*Your partner*
1 'Hello. I'm Charles.'	'Pleased to meet you.'
2 'Thanks!'	'You're welcome.'
3 'Do you like this picture?'	'Yes. It's lovely.'
4 'Anything else?'	'No, that's all, thank you.'
5 'Are you all right?'	'Yes, I'm fine.'

Now listen to your partner's sentences. What is the correct thing to say each time? Choose **a**, **b**, **c**, **d** or **e**.

a 'How do you do?'
b 'That's okay.'
c 'Fine, thanks.'
d 'Yes, that's right.'
e 'Yes, of course. go to the bank and turn left.'

Unit 13B   Exercise 4

Student B

1 Listen to **Student A** and fill in the ground floor map of Anita's school.

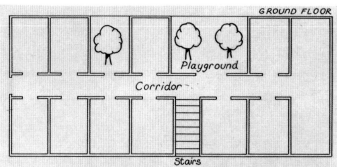

2 Now help **Student A** to fill in the first floor map of Anita's school.

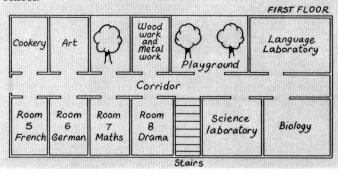

You are riding a bicycle.

Student C

Unit 7B Exercise 5

Unit 9B   Exercise 6

Student B

Look at the examples and the pictures. Write the questions.

1 *Example: Do you like playing tennis?*

2 *Example: What's your favourite colour?*

3 *Examples: Have you got any children? Have you got a camera?*

Answer your partner's questions. Now ask your partner the questions and make notes of the answers.

Unit 16B   Exercise 1

Student B

Listen to your partner and write one preposition in each space.

> My great uncle Ben, my grandfather's brother, emigrated
> _____ Argentina _____ 1919. He was the youngest son
> and only twenty. They lived _____ Wales and _____ that
> time there was no work, so many young men emigrated
> _____ the United States, Australia and South America. They
> didn't have much money, but the family saved enough
> _____ his boat fare. He was a farmer so he got work _____
> a sheep farm _____ Patagonia. He worked hard, saved his
> money and bought his own farm. He met the daughter
> _____ another immigrant _____ Wales and they got married
> and had children. He had a very good life and was a rich
> man when he died.

Now read this part of the text to your partner.

> He never came back to Wales, but he wrote to his
> family every week and sent photos. And last year
> his grandson, Thomas, visited us. It was strange because
> Thomas speaks Spanish of course, but he also speaks
> Welsh. So many people emigrated to Wales and they
> stayed together in Patagonia: they spoke Welsh and
> kept many of the Welsh customs. But one thing changed.
> Our name is James and in Argentina they say it
> the Spanish way – James – which sounds very funny
> to us.

Unit 18A   Exercise 2

Student B

> **Name:** Ross Gethin
> **Date of Birth:** 14 July 1973
> **Nationality:** British
> **Education and Qualifications:**
> St Paul's School, London
> 'A' levels in Biology, Mathematics and Chemistry 1989
> Durham University
> Degree in Business and Marketing 1992
> **Additional information:**
> My mother is Spanish so I am bilingual in Spanish and
> English. Every year I used to visit relatives in Madrid.

Unit 13A   Exercise 4

Student B

You have the names and descriptions of seven children in the photograph on page 87. Your partner has the names and descriptions of seven other children in the photograph.
Take turns to describe the children, and write their names in the correct places under the photograph. The girl *without* a description is Claire. Work with your partner and write a description of her.

Alex: light brown hair, yellow, white and blue striped T-shirt, shorts
Louise: long dark hair in a fringe and two plaits
Matthew: blonde hair with a straight fringe, blue eyes, red, black and blue striped T-shirt
Mark: curly brown hair, blue shirt
Judith: long brown hair with a fringe, blue T-shirt
Steve: brown hair, blue eyes, grey T-shirt
Patrick: dark hair, brown eyes, black T-shirt

Unit 18B   Exercise 4

Student B

You are Rosa Ayala. Your partner is Sara Gibson.
Look at your diary. Read your part in the dialogue on page 118 and then continue the conversation. Make suggestions and reply to your partner's suggestions. when you find a time you can meet say:
Yes. See you then. Bye.

MONDAY
P.M Bet Conference
TUESDAY

WEDNESDAY
P.M Meeting
THURSDAY 10 a.m I.H
P.M Bookshop.
FRIDAY

APESCRIPTS

Unit 1B   Exercise 1

Mary: Good morning!
Michel: Good morning! My name's Lebrun, Michel Lebrun.
Mary: Oh, yes. Mr Lebrun. Can you spell your surname, please?
Michel: *Capital L-e-b-r-u-n* ... Lebrun.
Mary: Thank you. And what's your nationality?
Michel: I'm French.
Mary: And your passport number, please?
Michel: Oh ... er ... it's, um 7-234829.
Mary: And what's your occupation?
Michel: I'm a teacher.
Mary: And your car number, please?
Michel: Er ... it's 26 78 NR 29.
Mary: And your address in France?
Michel: 9 rue Dupont, Landerneau.
Mary: Can you spell it, please?
Michel: Yes. It's 9 rue Dupont ... *r-u-e* ... *Capital D-u-p-o-n-t* ... rue Dupont. Landerneau ... *Capital L-a-n-d-e-r-n-e-a-u.*
Mary: Ah, Landerneau ... in Normandy?
Michel: No, we aren't from Normandy. Landerneau's in Brittany.
Mary: Oh ... Brittany. And your wife? What's her first name, please?
Michel: Her name's Marie ... Marie Lebrun.
Mary: Nationality French?
Michel: No, she isn't French. She's Canadian.
Mary: Oh, she isn't French. OK. Nationality Canadian. And, er ... children?
Michel: Yes, we have two children, Josephe and Patricia.
Mary: Can you spell their names?
Michel: OK. Josephe is *J-o-s-e-p-h-e.* Patricia is *P-a-t-r-i-c-i-a.*
Mary: Ages?
Michel: Patricia is five and, er, Josephe is eight.
Mary: OK. Now can I have your signature, please?
Michel: OK.
Mary: Thank you, Mr Lebrun. Have a good holiday!

Unit 1B   Exercise 2

John's father's name is Paul.
Paul is Kathleen's husband.
Kathleen is John's mother.
Helen is John's wife.
John and Helen have a son, Sam, and a daughter, Emily.
Sam and Emily are John's children.
Sam is Emily's brother and Emily is Sam's sister.
Helen has a sister, Edith.
Edith is Emily's aunt.
John has a brother, Tony.
Tony is Emily's uncle.
Helen's parents are Henry and Pamela.
Henry is Helen's father and Pamela is her mother.
Henry and Pamela are Sam's grandparents.
Henry is Sam's grandfather.
Pamela is Sam's grandmother.

Unit 1B   Exercise 4

1 *Helen:*   This is my husband, John. And our two children.

2 *John:*   This is our son, Sam. He's ten. And this is his sister. Her name's Emily and she's seven.

3 *Michel:* Hello, Sam. Hello, Emily.

4 *Michel:* This is our daughter, Patricia. She's five. And this is her brother. His name's Josephe and he's eight.

5 *Marie:*   Can I help?

6 *Emily:*   This is my friend. Her name's Patricia. She's from France.

Unit 2B   Exercise 1

1 'Excuse me. Where's the restaurant?'   'It's over there.'
   'And where's the meeting point?'   'It's here.'

2 'Excuse me. Where are the buses?'   'They're over there.'
   'And where are the toilets?'   'They're here.'

Unit 2B   Exercise 3

1 'How much is this, please?   'It's £28.00.'
2 'How much is that, please?   'It's £35.00.'
3 'How much are these, please?'   'They're 65 pence.'
4 'How much are those, please?'   'They're 50 pence.'
5 'How much is this, please?'   'It's £89.99.'
6 'How much is that, please?'   'It's £95.75.'
7 'How much are these, please?'   'They're £2.99.'
8 'How much are those, please?'   'They're £3.50.'

Unit 2B   Exercise 6

1 Smoking or non-smoking?
   Sorry?
   Smoking or non-smoking on the plane?
   Oh, non-smoking, please.

2 Oh, I'm sorry.
   It's OK.
   Can I get you another coffee?
   No, it's OK.

3 How much are those?
   Sorry?
   How much are those?
   Oh, they're 45p.

4 Ow!
   Oh, I'm sorry!
   It's OK, but be careful.
   Sorry.

5 Excuse me. Where are the buses for London?
   Sorry?
   Where are the buses for London?
   They're over there.
   Thank you.

6 Are you Mr Lewis?
   Sorry?
   Are you Mr Lewis?
   Yes, I am.

Unit 3B   Exercise 1

Elisabeth: Hello. Are you a new student? What's your name?
Ricardo: Ricardo. I'm from Spain.
Elisabeth: And my name's Elisabeth. I'm from Germany... Er ... my friend Elena comes from Spain.
Ricardo: Oh? Where in Spain?
Elisabeth: Barcelona. Where are you from?
Ricardo: Madrid. It's a nice city.
Elisabeth: Mmm... It is.

Ricardo: Do you like the college?
Elisabeth: Oh yes. I learn a lot and I like the lessons. We have a good teacher.
Ricardo: What do you do in the lessons?
Elisabeth: Oh ... a lot. We talk a lot. We read books and ... er ... newspapers. We listen to cassettes and we work with computers.
Ricardo: Do you learn English grammar?
Elisabeth: Yes, sometimes. It's difficult, but it's useful, I think.
Ricardo: And erm ... what time do the classes end?
Elisabeth: At er half past three.
Ricardo: And what do you do then?
Elisabeth: Ah, I work in the library for about an hour, and then I go home. Erm ... I have dinner with Mr and Mrs White and their children at about seven o'clock. That's very good for me ... a real English lesson! And then after dinner, erm ... I do my homework or I watch television or go out with my friends ...
Ricardo: And Saturday and Sunday?
Elisabeth: At the weekend? ... Well, you know, I go to a disco, or a party, or the cinema sometimes ...

Unit 4B   Exercise 1

Assistant: Can I help you?
Luigi: Can I have a phonecard, please?
Assistant: Anything else?
Luigi: No, that's all, thank you.

Luigi: Can I phone Italy?
Assistant: Yes, from the phone over there.
Luigi: Thank you.

Joanna: Pronto ...
Luigi: Hello, it's Luigi.
Joanna: Oh, hi. How are you?
Luigi: Fine, everything's fine. How are you? And the baby?
Joanna: We're OK.

Unit 4B   Exercise 3

a 'Hello? 226 8135?'

b 'Hello – is that 236 947?'

c 'Operator ... What number, please?'
   'Erm ... 3027, please.'

d 'Hello, this is 081 362 0054.
   I'm sorry I'm not at home, but please ...

e ... and my number is 0256 1093.'

Unit 5A   Exercise 4

1 Say 'good morning' in your language.
2 Write your signature.
3 Put your book in your bag.
4 Look at the window.
5 Turn to page 100 in your book...
6 ... and read the first sentence.
7 Look at the door.
8 Get your key and put it on the desk.

Unit 5B   Exercise 1

Barbara is at the clock tower between West Street and Queens Street:

Barbara: Excuse me! Can you tell me the way to the theatre, please?
Man: Yes. Go along North Street and turn left into New Road. The theatre's on your left opposite the coach park.
Barbara: Thank you!
Man: You're welcome!

George is at the clock tower between West Street and Queens Street:

George: Excuse me, can you tell me the way to the Hotel Metropole, please?
Woman: Er ... yeah .... go along West Street and turn left into Kings Road. Walk along Kings Road and the Hotel Metropole is on your right.
George: Thank you!
Woman: You're welcome!

George is in the Grand Parade opposite the Brighton Polytechnic of Arts:

George: Excuse me. Can you tell me the way to the market, please?
Woman: Yes, of course. Go along Grand Parade and turn right into Morley Street and the market is on your right.
George: Thank you!
Woman: You're welcome!

Barbara is outside the theatre in New Road:

Barbara: Excuse me. Can you tell me the way to the museum, please?
Man: Yes. go along this road. Then turn right into Church Street and walk along that street. The museum is on your right near the library.
Barbara: Thank you!
Man: You're welcome!

Unit 6A Exercise 1

Dr Manning: Well – this is the dining room where we have our meals. The meals are good.
Dr Li: Can I have breakfast here?
Dr Manning: Oh yes, breakfast, lunch, dinner ... and snacks too. Now we go outside ...
Dr Li: Ooh, it's cold.
Dr Manning: Yes, it is. Erm ... That's the car park – over there.
Dr Li: Oh, I cycle to work.
Dr Manning: Oh, me too. But you must be careful – we don't want you to have an accident!
Dr Li: Oh no!
Dr Manning: Now – this is the swimming pool.
Dr Li: Lovely! Can patients use the pool?
Dr Manning: No – it's for doctors, nurses and hospital workers. And this is the Sports Centre – there's a squash court – do you play squash?
Dr Li: Yes, I do. Do you?
Dr Manning: No, but I play tennis. Ah, inside again.
Dr Li: After you.
Dr Manning: Thank you. This is the library. It's a nice place to study.
Dr Li: Can I borrow books?
Dr Manning: Yes. You must get a library card from the librarian, then you can borrow books. And this is the Lounge. Erm ... you can read the newspapers and magazines, watch television ...
Dr Li: Mm ... it's very nice.
Dr Manning: And here are the shops ... the shops are for everyone ... patients, visitors, doctors, nurses ... You can buy everything here ... food, cards, stamps. There's a book shop over there where you can buy books ...
Dr Li: Oh yes.
Dr Manning: And here we are again in Reception.
Dr Li: Yes .,... well, thank you very much, Dr Manning.
Dr Manning: Oh – my name's Alison.
Dr Li: OK, Alison – my name's Joe.

Unit 6B Exercise 1

Woman: Look out! ...
... Yes, an ambulance, please. It's an accident, on Hills Road – at the Sports Centre ...
Policeman: Are you all right?
Simon: Oh, no – my arm hurts. I think it's broken ...
Policeman: Don't worry – here's the ambulance ...
Nurse: Hello. What's your name?
Simon: Simon Hebden.
Nurse: OK, Simon. Where does it hurt?
Simon: Oh, my arm, and my leg too ...

Unit Revision 1A Exercise 3

Go north along Panton Street. Take the second on the right and the first on the left. Then the first on the right. What can you see on your left?

Unit Revision 1B Exercise 1

Here is some information to help you. There's a map of the town on the desk in the study and a dictionary on the bookshelf. The car keys are on the kitchen table, but don't drive into the town centre. Parking is difficult and expensive. Go by bike – the bikes are in the garage.

Unit 7A Exercise 1

Hello and welcome to the start, on Staten Island, of the New York Marathon. There are 80 thousand people here today – men and women from 40 different countries ... about 5 million people are watching on television ... They're going down Fourth Avenue past Sunset Park ... It's a hot day and everyone is drinking a lot of water ... Hundreds of people are running over Queensboro Bridge ... Ahmed Ouita is in front – here he is in the red shorts – number 12 ... They're running along First Avenue now ... and over Willis Avenue Bridge ... They're going through the Bronx ... After 20 miles people are very tired ... a lot of people are walking now ... And here's Ahmed Ouita – he's coming over Madison Avenue Bridge ... now along Fifth Avenue past the Museum of the City of New York ... through Central Park to the finish ... Ahmed Ouita is the winner of the New York Marathon!

Unit 8A Exercise 1

Dorothea: Frank, this is Mr Vassilev from Bulgaria.
Frank: Pleased to meet you, Mr Vassilev.
Dorothea: Georg, meet Frank Miller from Britain.
Georg: How do you do.
Dorothea: Frank works for a big food company – Primo Supermarkets. Do you know them?
Georg: Yes, of course. Welcome to the Bulgarian stand, Mr Miller. How can I help you?
Frank: Erm ... I need some cheese for my company. What have you got?
Georg: Well, I've got some very good sheep's cheese. Here ... have some of this.
Frank: Mm ... it tastes delicious! Have a piece, Dorothea.
Dorothea: OK. Thanks ... Oh yes. It's very good.
Georg: Yes, it's good with bread or in a salad. In Bulgaria we make a salad with this cheese – Shopska salad.
Frank: Mm ... Well, I'm very interested in this cheese. And I hear you've got some very good walnuts too, Mr Vassilev.
Georg: Yes, we have. Here are some. Taste one.
Frank: Mm ... excellent! Can we meet later and discuss an order?
Georg: Certainly. What about lunch? Dorothea, you know some good restaurants, I'm sure.
Dorothea: Yes, of course. Let's meet here at half past one. There are some good restaurants ...

Unit 8B Exercise 1

Dorothea: Well, what are you having, Frank? Are you having a starter?
Frank: Yes. I'm having the er ... carrot and orange soup. What about you, Georg?
Georg: What do you suggest?

Dorothea:	Have some chicken liver paté. I'm having some. It's delicious.
Georg:	OK. Good idea. Now what about the main course? Frank?
Frank:	Mm ... Honey roast chicken for me, with a baked potato ... and vegetables. What about you?
Georg:	Er ... what is 'steak and onion pie?'
Frank:	Oh, it's steak and onion, baked in pastry.
Georg:	OK. Steak and onion pie for me then, with chips and erm ... vegetables. And for you Dorothea?
Dorothea:	Scottish salmon for me, with a baked potato and salad. And let's have a bottle of wine. White or red? Oh, here's the waiter.
Waiter:	Can I have your order now, sir?
Frank:	Of course ... What vegetables have you got today?
Waiter:	Er ... peas and cauliflower.
Frank:	Fine ...
Dorothea:	What about wine? Have you got any British wine?
Waiter:	No, madam. We haven't got any British wine. But we've got some very good French house wine ... white or red.
Dorothea:	OK. The red house wine then please. And can we have some water?
Georg:	Mm ... This is very good.
Frank:	Yes, delicious. What about a dessert now? Waiter, can we see the menu again, please? ... Thank you. Let's see now. Apple pie for me, I think. What about you, Dorothea?
Dorothea:	OK, fruit salad for me, please.
Georg:	And ... baked bananas for me, please. And coffee. A cup of black coffee. What about you two? Coffee?
Dorothea:	Oh yes, white for me please. Frank?
Frank:	Me too, please.
Georg:	And can we have the bill, please. Now, about that order, Frank ...

Unit 9A   Exercise 2

1   Here's Nicky, wearing a knee-length olive green dress in 100% wool. And under it, an orange polo neck cotton sweater. Nicky's wearing a matching orange hat.

2   Angela's wearing a royal blue short jacket over a black T-shirt, with matching blue trousers and a long red wool scarf.

3   Kim's wearing a white jacket, with a yellow silk scarf. The shoes and trousers are black, and Kim's also carrying a black jacket.

4   And here's Jasmin, wearing a long-sleeved white blouse with a long orange and brown skirt and matching brown shoes.

Unit 9A   Exercise 4

Interviewer:	You've got a clothes shop?
Jacquie:	Yes, I have ... in Dublin ... in Ireland.
Interviewer:	Ireland. So you're here in Milan, and you're ... er ... looking at the new clothes for spring?
Jacquie:	Yes, I am. I come to the fashion shows two or three times every year. I always come to Milan because ... er ... well, I like Italian clothes!

Interviewer:	And do you buy clothes at the show?
Jacquie:	Yes, I do ... well, sometimes I buy clothes at the show and sometimes I don't ...
Interviewer:	Do you buy clothes from other countries?
Jacquie:	Yes, I like German clothes and I buy a lot of clothes for young people and children, from England and Spain.
Interviewer:	Have you got any children?
Jacquie:	No, but I think I know what they like.
Interviewer:	And do you like the clothes at this year's show?
Jacquie:	Well, I like some of the women's clothes very much. This dress is very nice and I like those shoes. But ... well, I don't like the men's clothes very much this year.

Unit 9B   Exercise 2

Mum:	This jacket's nice.
Tom:	Oh mum – it's horrible!
Mum:	And I like these trousers.
Tom:	Ugh! I like those shoes. Can I have some new shoes?
Mum:	No, you can't – do you like that shirt?
Tom:	Oh, it's awful!
Mum:	Oh, Tom, do you like any of the clothes ... ?
Tom:	Yes, I like this sweater.
Mum:	Oh Tom!

Unit 10A   Exercise 1

Father:	So when are you leaving?
Jennifer:	Next Saturday. We're flying to New York, and then from New York to Tampa.
Father:	And where are you staying?
Jennifer:	On the West Coast, in St Petersburg, at the Beach Garden Hotel. It's quite cheap but it's got a swimming pool and it's near the beach.
Father:	Oh, that's good. It's very hot in Florida at this time of year. And are you staying in St Petersburg all the time?
Jennifer:	No, We're spending a week there from Saturday to Saturday – and then a week in Orlando. We're planning a visit to Disneyworld there.
Father:	How are you getting from St Petersburg to Orlando? Are you flying?
Jennifer:	No. It's not far; it's only about two hours away. We're hiring a car for those two weeks. We want to drive around and see as much as possible.
Father:	What do you want to see?
Jennifer:	... oh, lots of places. There's ...

Unit 10B   Exercise 4

1   OK. Goodbye then. See you later.
     Bye ... Oh look! My umbrella ... I need my umbrella.

2   The weather's bad today.
     Yes, just listen to it.

3   Let's sit in the garden.
     Good idea. Where are my sunglasses?

4   Nice day today.
     Yes, better than yesterday – warmer. How's your mother ...?

5 The temperature in Orlando this morning is 39° centigrade! Wow ... get the cold drinks ready!

6 Brrr! Look at the weather!
Yeah ... everything's white. Oh, I want to stay at home! – it's nice and warm inside.

Unit 11A   Exercise 1

Receptionist: Welcome to the Conference.
Karin Jagge: Thank you.
Frederik Jagge: Thank you.
Receptionist: Now – can we fill in the registration forms?
Karin Jagge: Yes, of course.
Receptionist: First, can I have your name, madam?
Karin Jagge: Yes, my name's Karin Jagge – that's *K-a-r-i-n* for the first name.
Receptionist: *K-a-r-i-n* ...
Karin Jagge: ... and then Jagge – that's *J-a-double g-e*.
Receptionist: ... *J-a-double g*?
Karin Jagge: Yes.
Receptionist: ...-*e*.
Karin Jagge: That's right.
Receptionist: And where are you from, Mrs Jagge?
Frederik Jagge: Acdtually it's Doctor Jagge.
Receptionist: Oh, sorry.
Karin Jagge: It's all right. I'm from Norway.
Receptionist: So – Norwegian.
Karin Jagge: That's right.
Receptionist: Can I have the name of your university or institution?
Karin Jagge: Yes, Oslo University.
Receptionist: OK. Now, are you giving a talk at the conference?
Karin Jagge: Yes, I am, on Wednesday.
Receptionist: And are you going to the conference dinner?
Karin Jagge: Oh, when is it?
Receptionist: On Wednesday evening.
Karin Jagge: Oh, yes – Frederik? What do you think?
Frederik Jagge: Oh yes, of course.
Receptionist: Good – that's everything. The room for you and your husband is number 35.
Karin Jagge: Thank you.
Receptionist: Can we fill in the form for you, sir, then someone can help you with your bags.
Frederik Jagge: Fine. My name's Frederik ...

Unit 11A   Exercise 4

Peter: Hello, Karen.
Karen: Oh hi, Peter.
Peter: How are you?
Karen: Fine, how are you?
Peter: Oh, fine.
Er .. when are you giving your talk?
Karen: *
Peter: Oh, that's at the same time as mine.
Karen: Really? But where's your talk?
Peter: *
Karen: Oh, that's bigger than my room – so more people!
Peter: Why? Where are you giving your talk?
Karen: *

Peter: I see.
Karen: Are you talking about your work in Central Europe?
Peter: *
And what about you? What are you giving a talk about?
Karen: *
Peter: That's interesting. I'm sorry it's at the same time as mine! Are you going to the Wildlife in Africa Exhibition?
Karen: Oh, I don't know. When is it?
Peter: *
Karen: Mmm. Probably not. It's right after my talk – and yours!
Peter: Mmm.
Karen: What about the dinner – are you going to the conference dinner?
Peter: When is it?
Karen: *
Peter: Yes, probably. What about you – are you going?
Karen: *
Peter: Well, I must go. See you.
Karen: Yes, see you later, bye!

Unit 11B   Exercise 4

1 How are you?
2 I'm fine.
3 How are you?
4 What are you doing?
5 I'm working at the Sorbonne.
6 What's Paris like?
7 How's your little boy?
8 We've got two boys now.
9 Which talks are you going to?
10 I don't know.

Unit 11B   Exercise 6

1 I think okra is awful.
Oh, I don't. I like it.

2 I think the food in America is very good.
No! How can you say that?

3 I really think the tiger is in danger.
Yes, I think you're right.

4 I think Paulo's doing very good work at the university.
Yes, perhaps you're right.

5 I think this is a very good conference.
Yes, so do I.

6 I think Kenya is great.
Yes, but it's very hot!

Unit 11B   Exercise 8

1 This animal is very big. It's grey. It comes from Africa and India. It's got a long nose called a trunk.

2 This animal is brown and white. It comes from Africa. It's got a long neck. It's very tall.

3 This animal is brown. It can jump. It comes from Australia. It carries its babies in a pocket called a pouch.

4 This is a small animal. It can be brown or white. It has long ears. It has a small white tail.

5 This animal is a big cat. It's usually bigger than a dog, but smaller than a horse. It comes from India. It's got black and yellow stripes.

Unit 12A   Exercise 2

Welcome to sunny Tokyo. It's four o'clock in the afternoon here on Wednesday, the fifth of June, a very hot day, the day of the final of the women's 200 metres. And we can see the runners now – they're warming up with a minute to go before the start. There's the favourite to win this race, the American, Jill Washington. She's wearing number 6. And that's the Mexican, Olivia Pizarro, wearing number 3, and there's the Irish runner, Linda Casey, wearing number 4. And they're lining up now. The Kenyan runner, Martha Mbene, is number 2. There's number 5, Betty Diamond from Australia, and number 1, Monica Gutholf from Norway. And they're off! Good start there, and they're running well. Washington and Casey are in front, and they're running together now and ... no, Casey is running past Washington! And Casey's out in front ... and here comes Mbene and Gutholf – they're overtaking Washington and Washington is in the fourth position now. But Casey is finishing strongly, and Casey's the winner with Mbene in second place and Gutholf in third place! The Irish runner Linda Casey, is the winner of the women's 200 metres! A great race! And there's the winner, she's waving and smiling happily – it's a great day for her. And there's Jill Washington, the woman in fourth position, watching sadly. She's walking away slowly now. No medal for her this year. But a bronze medal for Monica Gutholf, a silver medal for Martha Mbene and gold for Linda Casey. This is John Birch handing you back to the BBC studios in London.

Unit 12B   Exercise 1

Hello? Mum, is that you? Yeah, it's me, Linda. How are you? And how's Dad? Did you have a good party? I heard you were up all night. Yeah? really? Oh yeah, it's great here! We had a party too – yeah, we went to the Hilton to celebrate. They made a big cake. It was great. What? The medals? Oh yeah ... they gave us the medals yesterday. Did you see it on television? Good. Yeah, it was wonderful. Michael wrote me a letter. He said he spoke to you on the phone. Yeah. He said you were delighted. Yeah ... okay ... okay, yeah. Listen ... I must go now. Yeah. See you soon. Okay ... Bye.

Revision 2A   Exercise 3

Tiina: People think, because I'm a model I don't eat very much. But I do! I like fruit and vegetables, and ... er ... pasta, rice, eggs – lots of things. I don't eat red meat but I like chicken and fish sometimes. I eat the food of the country I'm working in. I like all kinds of food – Italian, Chinese, French, Indian – anything really. I must be careful about some food – I don't eat cakes or pastry or ice cream – that kind of food. But sometimes I have some chocolate – I love it! Drinks? Well, lots of water, because that's good for you – and tea. I don't like alcohol ... or coffee.

Carlos: For my sport I eat a lot – OK I'm driving – but I, it's hard work. And I run 15 kilometres every day. I like rice,

beans, meat and cheese. I travel a lot – a different country every month – so I eat food from all over the world. I like fruit and I drink a lot of fruit juice. And I drink a lot of water – I always drink a lot before a race – it's thirsty work! Really, my favourite food is – it's the food my mother makes – food from Argentina.

Revision 2B   Exercise 1

Here we are in Florida. The weather's hot but it rains a lot too. We go swimming every day in the hotel pool. Tomorrow we're going to Disneyworld. We're arriving early and spending all day there. On Wednesday we're visiting Universal Studios. We want to see the places from famous films. We're flying back on Friday. See you then.

Unit 13A   Exercise 2

1 When she was five years old Claire lived with her grandparents.
2 She walked one and a half kilometres to school every day.
3 When they arrived at school, Claire's mother stopped.
4 Her friend, Anthony, wanted to play with boys, not with Claire.
5 Her teacher smiled and seemed friendly.
6 Claire liked reading but she hated maths.

Unit 13B   Exercise 2

1 Now listen carefully, class two. Triangle ABC has got three equal sides. What do we call this kind of triangle?

2 OK ... now, as you know, animals breathe in oxygen and breathe out carbon dioxide. But what about plants? What do they do?

3 In 1066 William of Normandy invaded Britain. He won the Battle of Hastings and became King William I of England. After that a lot of Normans came to Britain and made it their home.

4 In the last lesson we spoke about maps and how people make maps. And for homework you made your own maps of the way you come to school.

Unit 13A   Exercise 3

My first day at school? Yeah, I can remember it quite well really. Erm ... I was five when I started school and I very much wanted to go to school because my older brother was already at school. I walked. I walked with my mother. It was only about five minutes from my house. Erm ... and the buildings ... were rather small little buildings ... Erm ... and I remember that they smelled funny. They smelled of disinfectant and other children. And the class seemed to me to be full of lots of big children – I think probably there were only about twenty-six people in my class but it seemed very big, er and a lot of them were older than me. And I was very, very shy. Erm ... it was rather disappointing actually because I was too afraid to speak to anybody ... so ... I don't think I said anything to anybody all day long. I can remember drawing pictures, and I was sitting next to a girl called Gillian who had a very big nose ... My teacher was called Miss Finney and she was very fat. I didn't like her very much I don't think. I was afraid of her too... Erm ... and I didn't really make any friends. There was a boy called Stephen who I was friendly with later but certainly not on the first day. I don't think I did enjoy my first day very much because nobody talked to me and ... and I didn't learn to read on the first day. I wanted to learn to read. Of course I didn't learn to read on the first day I was there. It's the morning I remember, I think. I can't remember the afternoon very much. Mm ... and that's about all I can remember really.

Unit 14A   Exercise 3

Well, I started university on a Saturday. I knew only one person at the university – it was someone from home – his name was Ian. It was Ian's third year at university and he had a lot of friends. In my first week I made friends with a girl called Sara. Then Ian invited me to a restaurant to meet some of his friends the next Saturday. So I went with Sara to the restaurant to meet them. Well, we got a drink and some food and sat down and talked. And after about an hour I looked up and I saw a young man come into the restaurant. I didn't know the man but I suddenly felt very funny and I said to Sara, 'That's the man I'm going to marry.' I was lucky because Ian knew the young man and he introduced him. And that was 28 years ago. It's our 25th wedding anniversary this year.

Unit 14B   Exercise 1

Diane: Andrea, when are you getting married?
Andrea: I'm getting married on the 11th of July.
Diane: Hmm, OK, and where are you getting married?
Andrea: In Budapest in ...
Diane: Are you getting married in a church?
Andrea: Well, yes. We first have to go to a register's office and then go to a small church.
Diane: OK. And what are you going to wear?
Andrea: I'm going to wear a wedding dress, erm ...
Diane: What colour?
Andrea: Erm ... white, a long wedding dress.
Diane: Are you going to carry anything?
Andrea: Erm ... probably a bunch of flowers.
Diane: And what's Zoltan going to wear?
Andrea: He's going to wear a dinner jacket.
Diane: And is Zoltan going to wear a wedding ring?
Andrea: Yes, he will.
Diane: And what's going to happen after the wedding?
Andrea: After the wedding there's going to be a reception.
Diane: Hmm ... With lots of people?
Andrea: Probably ... we sent a hundred invitation cards so ..
Diane: That's a lot! And after you're married where are you going to live?
Andrea: Erm ... We're going to live with my parents.

Unit 15A   Exercise 1

Joanna: Hello. I'm Joanna. Are you Lucy?
Lucy: Yes. Hello Joanna. You phoned about the room, didn't you? Come in. This is Daniel. We share the flat, and we're looking for someone for the third bedroom.
Joanna: Hello, Daniel. Pleased to meet you!
Daniel: Hi, Joanna. Would you like a cup of coffee?
Joanna: Oh, yes please.
Daniel: Black or white?
Joanna: White please. No sugar.
Lucy: Okay ... well, come and see the room first and then we can have our coffee. This is the bathroom.

Daniel: So ... there's your coffee.
Joanna: Thanks. That's lovely.
Daniel: And there's yours, Lucy.
Lucy: Thanks, Daniel ... Daniel is an actor but he makes some extra money working in a café. That's why he makes good coffee.
Joanna: I see. And what about you, Lucy? What do you do?
Lucy: Me? Oh, I work in a bank. It's not very exciting but the money isn't bad. ... Anyway, what about the room? What do you think of it?
Joanna: It's very nice. The rent is £60 a week, isn't it?
Lucy: Yes, that's right. But we have to pay extra for heating, electricity and the telephone.
Joanna: How much do you have to pay for that?
Daniel: Oh, it usually comes to about £10 a week.
Joanna: Mm ... well, I'm a student nurse, so I'm not exactly rich! But my parents help me a bit, and it's very near the hospital ... Er, what about the neighbours? Are they noisy? Sometimes I have to work at night and sleep in the daytime, so my room has to be quiet.
Lucy: Oh, it's very quiet during the day here. Most people are out at work all day. One lady on the ground floor has got a dog, but it's very quiet. We never hear it, do we, Daniel?
Daniel: No, it's very quiet. Of course, when we play our music in the evenings ...
Joanna: Well, I like it here a lot, so ... er ... if it's okay with you ...
Lucy: Great!
Daniel: That's fine! When are you going to move in?

Unit 15B   Exercise 2

Lucy: Listen, you two. We must talk about the party on Saturday.
Daniel: Yeah ... okay. What do we have to do for the party?
Joanna: Well ... erm ... we have to buy the food on Friday, so we can cook it on Saturday.
Daniel: Yes ... and we mustn't forget to buy some decorations ... you know, candles and balloons and things.
Lucy: Oh yes, that's right, and we have to clean the flat and put up the decorations on Saturday. We're going to be busy!
Joanna: What about the music?
Lucy: Oh, that's okay. We don't have to worry about the music. My friend, Malcolm, is bringing his tapes with him.
Daniel: Good, but we mustn't play the music too loud after 11 o'clock. We don't want Mrs Crossley upstairs to phone the police, do we?
Joanna: And glasses? I don't think ... erm ... we haven't got enough glasses, have we?
Daniel: Oh yes ... I forgot to tell you ... The man in the shop on the corner is going to lend us some glasses. We're going to buy a lot of drinks from him so we don't have to pay for the glasses.
Lucy: Okay ... that's great. I can't wait for Saturday!

Unit 16A Exercise 1

1 What is the name of this statue?
2 Where is it?
3 Who gave the statue to the people of the United States?
4 When did they give the statue?
5 How tall is the statue?
6 What is the statue made of?
7 How many people visit the statue each year?

Unit 16B Exercise 1

My great Uncle Ben, my grandfather's brother, emigrated to
Argentina in 1919. He was the youngest son and only twenty.
They lived in Wales and at that time there was no work, so many
young men emigrated to the United States, Australia and South
America. They didn't have much money but the family saved
enough for his boat fare. He was a farmer so he got work on a
sheep farm in Patagonia. He worked hard, saved his money and
bought his own farm. He met the daughter of another immigrant
from Wales and they got married and had children. He had a very
good life and was a rich man when he died. He never came back to
Wales but he wrote to his family every week and last year his
grandson, Thomas, visited us. It was strange because Thomas
speaks Spanish of course, but he also speaks Welsh. So many
people emigrated from Wales and they stayed together in
Patagonia: they spoke Welsh and kept many of the Welsh customs.
But one thing changed. Our name is James and in Argentina they
say it the Spanish way – James – which seems very funny to us.

Unit 16B Exercise 4

Interviewer: When did you immigrate to Britain?
Shaheen: Well, I was only two when my family emigrated from
Pakistan – it was thirty years ago, so of course I don't
remember Pakistan.
Interviewer: So you were born in Pakistan?
Shaheen: Yes, but I'm British now – all my family are British
citizens.
Interviewer: What did your father do?
Shaheen: In Pakistan he was a teacher but when he came to
Britain he started his own business.
Interviewer: And your mother?
Shaheen: Oh, she stayed at home with the children.
Interviewer: Did your father speak good English?
Shaheen: Yes, he learned very quickly. He went to evening
school and he studied hard, with grammar books and
dictionaries. But it was harder for my mother. Where
we lived, everyone was from Pakistan. She didn't
have to learn English – there were Pakistani shops,
Pakistani doctors, Pakistani cinemas ...
Interviewer: But you learned English at school.
Shaheen: Yes, I learned very quickly at school from the other
children and I watched television and I read a lot -
stories, magazines ...
Interviewer: What was the hardest thing for you?
Shaheen: My mother didn't want me to play with the other
children after school. I had to go home and help my
mother. When I was older I didn't have boyfriends.
My father wanted me to marry a man from Pakistan.
He wanted to choose my husband.

Interviewer: And did he choose your husband?
Shaheen: No, I met my husband at Medical School. He's a
doctor, like me.
Interviewer: Was your father very angry?
Shaheen: No, because my husband's family are from Pakistan.
They emigrated in 1975. He comes from a good
family. So it was OK.
Interviewer: Do you work?
Shaheen: Yes, I'm a doctor. I work at the City Hospital.
Interviewer: And have you got any children?
Shaheen: Yes, I have a little girl.
Interviewer: Do you speak English at home?
Shaheen: Yes, of course – we are very English! My daughter's
life is very different from mine.
Interviewer: And your life is very different from your mother's
life.
Shaheen: Yes, very different!

Unit 17A Exercise 2

Richard: Now, Fred, a year ago you won £500,000. Is your life
very different now from what it was?
Fred: Oh yes, very different. When I was a dustman I used to
get up early and do the same boring job every day. But
now ... er ... well, I get up when I want to and I do what I
want to. My life is much more interesting now.
Richard: Why? What do you do with your time now?
Fred: Well, I've got some new friends and we meet ... er ... and
sometimes we go out together. I go to the races quite a lot
... you know ... horse-racing ... And my wife and I, we
travel a lot now too. We always used to go to Southend
for a holiday, but last year we went to Greece and Spain.
In fact, I'm learning Spanish at evening classes.
Richard: Really? What's that like?
Fred: Well, it's quite difficult really, and ... er ... it's more
difficult for me, I think, than for a lot of people, because I
didn't learn a language when I was at school.
Richard: What about other changes, Fred?
Fred: Other changes? ...Er ...Well, of course, there's this house.
We used to live in a small flat in north-east London ... It
wasn't ours, you know, we rented it. But when we won
the lottery we bought this house in the country. Oh, it's
wonderful ... it's got five bedrooms, you know, and three
bathrooms. We're much more comfortable now than we
were.
Richard: Yes, I can see that. It's a lovely house, Fred. And what
about your wife. Does she like her new life?
Fred: She certainly does, Richard, yes ... yes, she does ... well,
er, she doesn't have to clean for other people any more,
does she? In fact, she doesn't have to clean at all ...
someone comes in and cleans for us now! So yeah, Alice
used to work very hard, but she can take it easy now.
Richard: One last question, Fred. What's the most enjoyable thing
about your life now?
Fred: Oh, that's easy. I don't have to do dirty work and I can
have a bath as often as I want to. When I was a dustman I
used to get dirty and my clothes used to smell ... I hated
it. Now I've got a wonderful bathroom with gold taps and
a very big bath and as much hot water as I need. I enjoy
having a bath so much, I sometimes have two or three a
day!

Unit 17B Exercise 4

A: What's the most delicious food in the world?

B: Mm ... I think pizza is the most delicious food.

C: What about caviar?

D: That's the most expensive food in the world.

B: Okay ... my turn. Who's the friendliest person in your street?

C: Er ... Well, there's Carmelita at number 56 ... she's very friendly, she has lots of parties. What about in your street?

D: I don't live in a street ... I live in the country.

A: Who's the friendliest person in your family then?

D: Oh ... er ... that's probably my oldest brother ... he's got lots of friends.

Unit 18A Exercise 4

Part A

Ray: Good morning, Miss Gibson. Please sit down. I'm Ray Martin and this is Jane Thomson.

Sara: How do you do?

Jane: How do you do?

Ray: Now can I check a few things first?

Sara: Yes, of course.

Ray: Where did you go to school?

Sara: *

Ray: And when did you do your 'A' levels?

Sara: *

Ray: Did you study Spanish for 'A' level?

Sara: *

Ray: And which languages did you study at University?

Sara: *

Ray: Do you know any Catalan?

Part B

Ray: Now Mr Gethin, my colleague Jane Thomson is going to ask you some questions.

Ross: Fine.

Jane: Did you study languages at school or university?

Ross: *

Jane: But you speak Spanish?

Ross: *

Jane: And, er ... where did you go to university?

Ross: *

Jane: And what did you study at university?

Part C

Ray: Why do you want to do this job, Miss Gibson?

Sara: Well, I'm interested in books. I know about English language books because on my teacher training course we looked at a lot of books, and I used some when I taught English, so I know what the students like, too. I like meeting people – I like talking to people. Also, of course, I know Barcelona well, because I used to live there and I liked the city and the people very much. I'd like to learn more Catalan.

Jane: Have you any questions for us?

Sara: Yes, do most of the English teachers in the region speak Catalan or Spanish?

Jane: Well, a lot speak Catalan and ....

Jane: Why do you want this job, Mr Gethin?

Ross: I don't know really. I don't know much about books, especially English language books, but the job's in Barcelona and I know that's a really nice place – good shops, restaurants, beaches, that sort of thing, you know. And I'm sure I can do the job okay.

Ray: Yes, well ... er, and do you have any questions for us?

Ross: Yes, how much holiday does the Marketing Assistant get?

Ray: Well, for the first few months ....

Part D

Jane: Well, what do you think?

Ray: Let's look at Ross Gethin first. Appearance ... hmm ...

Jane: Okay, I suppose. Let's say 'satisfactory'.

Ray: I didn't like his long hair, but okay, satisfactory.

Jane: Now, education and qualifications. Well, he did sciences at 'A' level, not languages ...

Ray: Yes, but the degree in business and marketing is very useful, and he speaks fluent Spanish.

Jane: Yes, I agree. Let's put 'very good'.

Ray: Yes. Now, experience of the country – 'very good', but of books, 'not satisfactory'. He said he doesn't know anything about books.

Jane: Yes, and of marketing ... well, he has his degree in marketing ...

Ray: Yes, but no real experience. 'Satisfactory,' I think.

Jane: Yes, 'satisfactory'. Now, personality and attitude ...

Ray: Mmm ... not very good. I don't think he's interested in the job ...

Jane: He's just interested in having a holiday in Barcelona!

Ray: So ... 'not satisfactory'?

Jane: Yes, I think so.

Ray: Now, Sara ... a nice, friendly young woman ...

Jane: Yes, I liked her very much ... very good appearance ....

Ray: Yes, I agree. Let's put 'very good' for appearance.

Jane: And her education and qualifications are also excellent ...

Ray: Yes, 'very good' for that too.

Jane: Now, experience ...

Ray: Well, no problem with experience of the country – she lived in Barcelona for a year and she speaks some Catalan ...

Jane: Yes, so 'very good'...

Ray: And her experience of books is very good, too.

Jane: Yes, she used to work in the University Library in her school holidays, and the teaching qualification and experience teaching English is very useful too.

Ray: Yes, she knows something about English language books, so 'very good' for that?

Jane: Yes. Now, marketing. She's got no experience of marketing ...

Ray: No, we've got to put 'not satisfactory' for that.

Jane: Yes ... but her personality and attitude – excellent!

Ray: Yes, she was very enthusiastic, and she asked some very good questions ...

Jane: So I think we agree – Sara for the job?

Ray: Yes, let's offer her the job. Can you ask her to come in?

Unit 18 B   Exercise 1

Okay, welcome to our office. That's your desk, over there, and that's mine near the window – the one with all the papers! Do you like the yellow phone? You and I share a computer – the one in the corner – and we use the photocopier next door. You can get a drink at the drinks machine any time you want. We each have our own mugs – mine's the red one. Now over there ...

Unit 18B   Exercise 2

1 That's my desk.
2 That one's Sara's.
3 Can I use the fax machine?
4 Which is his mug?
5 It's next door.
6 The one in the corner.

Unit 18 B   Exercise 5

Okay, it's quite easy really – put the paper in here, this way round. press a button, here, for the number you want – and then press this green button. You can enlarge or reduce – use this button to enlarge and this one to reduce. Any problems – ask me or Jane. OK?

Revision Unit 3 A   Exercise 2

1   Well, she's very pretty.
2   I think she's got a very difficult job.
3   She wears lovely clothes – she always looks wonderful.
4   I think she's a very unhappy person.
5   She's got a lovely smile.
6   Well, she doesn't have to cook or do the cleaning – I think she's lucky.
7   She is always friendly.
8   I think her life must be very boring.
9   She's always kind to old people or people in hospital.
10 Well, she's not very clever, is she?
11 She always has to look her best.
12 She's a very good mother.

Revision Unit 3 B   Exercise 1

The wedding usually starts on a Wednesday and finishes on a Friday. The bride and bridegroom invite their friends and neighbours to the wedding and everyone wears new clothes. They have delicious food and there is dancing. One big difference between a wedding in a Western country and a wedding in my country is that there is no mixing between men and women at the wedding.

WORDLIST

A

ability *(n)* 6
about *(adv, approx)* 2
abroad *(adv)* 17
accident *(n)* 6
accountant *(n)* 3
actor *(n)* 4
actually *(adv)* 9
address *(n)* 1
adult *(n)* 18
advantage *(n)* 18
after *(prep)* 3
afternoon *(n)* 3
again 6
age *(n)* 1
airport *(n)* 2
alcohol *(n)* 7
all right *(adj)* 6
alligator *(n)* 10
alone *(adv)* 17
along *(prep)* 5
alphabet *(n)* 1
already *(adv)* 13
always *(adv)* 9
ambulance *(n)* 6
angry *(adj)* 16
animal *(n)* 10
anniversary *(n)* 14
another 2

answer *(n)* 1
any 8
appear *(v)* 17
apple *(n)* 7
applicant *(n)* 18
apply *(v)* 18
appointment *(n)* 18
archeology *(n)* 13
arm *(n)* 6
around *(adv)* 10
arrange *(v)* 15
arrival *(n)* 2
arrive *(v)* 10
art *(n)* 13
article *(n)* 9
artist *(n)* 10
ask *(v)* 1
assistant *(n)* 18
at *(prep)* 3
aunt *(n)* 1
available *(adj)* 4
award *(n)* 9
awful *(adj)* 9

B

baby *(n)* 4
back *(adv)* 10 *(n)* 6
bad *(adj)* 10
badly *(adv)* 12

bag *(n)* 2
baker *(n)* 5
balloon *(n)* 15
banana *(n)* 7
bank *(n)* 2
basket ball *(n)* 12
bath *(n)* 3
bathroom *(n)* 3
beach *(n)* 10
bean *(n)* 7
because 8
bed *(n)* 3
bedroom *(n)* 3
before *(prep)* 7
begin *(v)* 9
bell *(n)* 6
belong *(v)* 14
belt *(n)* 9
big *(adj)* 5
bike *(n)* 5
bill *(n)* 8
biology *(n)* 12
bird *(n)* 6
boat *(n)* 10
body *(n)* 6
blonde *(adj)* 13
boat *(n)* 10
body *(n)* 6
book *(n)* 4

book shop 6
boring *(adj)* 11
born *(be born, v)* 16
borrow *(v)* 6
bottle *(n)* 8
box *(n)* 14
boyfriend *(n)* 16
bread *(n)* 7
breakfast *(n)*
bride *(n)* 14
bridegroom *(n)* 14
bring *(v)* 15
brochure *(n)* 10
broken *(adj)* 6
bronze *(n)* 12
brother *(n)* 1
brown *(adj)* 9
building *(n)* 16
bus *(n)* 2
business *(n)* 12
busy *(adj)* 15
butcher *(n)* 5
button *(n)* 18
buy *(v)* 4
by *(prep)* 5

C

cafe *(n)* 15
camera *(n)* 2

camping *(n)* 1
can *(v)* 1
candle *(n)* 15
capital *(adj)* 1
car *(n)* 1
card *(n)* 4
careful *(adj)* 2
careless *(adj)* 13
carrot *(n)* 8
carry *(v)* 9
cat *(n)* 5
cauliflower *(n)* 8
centigrade *(n)* 10
cereal *(n)* 7
certainly 8
chair *(n)* 3
change *(n)* 17 *(v)* 16
cheap *(adj)* 10
check *(adj)* 10
cheese *(n)* 7
chemist *(n)* 5
chemistry *(n)* 12
cheque *(n)* 4
chicken *(n)* 7
child/children *(n)* 1
chips *(n)* 8
chocolate *(n)* 8
choose *(v)* 9
chop *(v)* 8

chubby *(adj)* 13
church *(n)* 14
cinema *(n)* 4
citizen *(n)* 16
city *(n)* 4
city centre *(n)* 4
class *(n)* 3
classical *(adj)* 9
classroom *(n)* 3
clean *(v)* 15
cleaner *(n)* 17
close *(v)* 9
clothes *(n)* 9
coach *(n)* 5
coast *(n)* 10
code *(n)* 4
coffee *(n)* 2
cold *(adj)* 6
colleague *(n)* 11
college *(n)* 3
colour *(n)* 9
colourful *(adj)* 10
comb *(v)* 13
come *(v)* 3
come up to *(v)* 13
comfortable *(adj)* 17
compact disc *(n)* 14
company *(n)* 8
competition *(n)* 17

note (n) 7
notice (n) 15
now (adv) 2
number (n) 1
nurse (n) 6

O

occupation (n) 1
of (prep) 2
of course 8
offer (v) 4
old (adj) 12
olive oil (n) 8
omelette (n) 8
on (prep) 2
onion (n) 7
only (adv) 6
open (adj) 4
opinion (n) 11
opposite (prep) 5
optional (adj) 11
orange (adj) 12 (n) 8
orchestra (n) 4
order (n) 8
other (adj) 9
outside (adv) 6
oven (n) 5
over (prep) 8
own (v) 16
owner (n) 5

P

panda (n) 11
paper (n) 3
parade (n) 10
parent (n) 1
park (n) 10
parking (n) 15
partner (n) 1
party (n) 15
passport (n) 1
passport control (n) 2
past (prep) 7
pasta (n) 8
pastry (n) 8
paté (n) 8
patient (n) 6
pavement (n) 6
pay (v) 17
pea (n) 8
peach (n) 7
pear (n) 7
pen (n) 3
pencil (n) 3
people (n) 9
pepper (n) 7,8
perfect (adj) 4
per night, person 4
permission (n) 4
person (n) 11
personality (n) 18
phone (n) 4
photocopier (n) 18
photograph (n) 4
photographer (n) 2

pick up (v) 10
picture (n) 1
pie (n) 8
piece (n) 8
place (n) 12
plan (v, n) 3, 10
plane (n) 2
plant (n) 15
plastic (n) 14
play (n) 4 (v) 6, 15
playground (n) 13
please 2
pocket (n) 11
police (n) 5
poor (adj) 16
pop music (n) 9
position (n) 12
possible (adj) 10
postcard (n) 4
potato (n) 7
practise (v) 1
press (v) 18
pretty (adj) 14
price (n) 8
printer (n) 18
product (n) 8
programme (n) 4
publisher (n) 18
put (v) 4
put on (v) 7
put up (v) 15

Q

qualification (n) 18
question (n) 1
quickly (adv) 12
quiet (adj) 15

R

rabbit (n) 11
race (n) 12
radio (n) 3
rain (v) 10
read (v) 1
reason (n) 16
reception (n) 4,14
receptionist (n) 4
red (adj) 8
reduce (v) 18
registration (n) 11
registry office (n) 14
relative (n) 16
remember (v) 13
rent (n) 15
repair (v) 14
repeat (v) 1
reply (v) 18
report (news) (n) 12
reporter (n) 12
request (n) 4
research (n) 11
restaurant (n) 2
result (n) 12
return (v, tr) 10
rice (n) 7

rich (adj) 15
ride (n) 10 (v) 6
right (adj) 4 (adv) 5
ring (n) 14
river (n) 16
road (n) 5
roast (adj) 8
room (n) 3
route (n) 7
royal (adj) 4
rubber (n) 3
ruler (n) 3
run (v) 6
run off (v) 13
runner (n) 12

S

sad (adj) 12
sadly (adv) 12
safe (adj) 16
salad (n) 7
salmon (n) 8
salt (n) 8
same 11
sandwich (n) 7
satisfactory (adj) 18
Saturday 3
save (v) 16
say (v) 1
scarf (n) 9
school (n) 3
science (n) 13
sea (n) 10
see (v) 4
sell (v) 4
send (v) 5
sentence (n) 11
service (n) 4
share (v) 14
shed (n) 5
sheep (n) 8
shine (v) 10
shirt (n) 9
shoe (n) 9
shop (n) 2
shopping (n) 15
short (adj) 13
shorts (n) 7
show (n) 4
shower (n) 3
signature (n) 1
silence (n) 6
silk (n) 9
silver (n) 12
singer (n) 9
single room (n) 4
sister (n) 1
sit (v) 10
size (n) 9
ski (v) 14
skirt (n) 9
sleep (v) 5
slim (adj) 13
slow (adj) 12
slowly (adv) 12

small (adj) 9
smell (v) 14
smile (v) 13
smoke (v) 2
snack bar (n) 2
social worker (n) 16
socialise (v) 11
some 8
sometimes (adv) 7
son (n) 1
sorry 2
soup (n) 8
south (adj) 10 (n) 5
souvenir (n) 4
speak (v) 1
spell (v) 1
spend (v) 10
sports centre (n) 6
spring (season) (n) 9
squash (court) (n) 6
stairs (n) 5
stamp (n) 4
stand (n) 8
stapler (n) 3
star (n) 12 (v) 17
start (n) 7 (v) 6
starter (n) 8
state (n) 16
station (n) 5
stay (v) 10
steak (n) 8
stone (n) 16
stop (v) 6
story (n) 7
strange (adj) 16
street (n) 5
stripe (n) 11
strong (adj) 12
strongly (adv) 12
student (n) 2
student games (n) 12
studio (n) 12
study (n) 3 (v) 7
successful (adj) 16
suddenly (adv) 13
sugar (n) 15
suggest (v) 8
suitable (adj) 18
summary (n) 9
sun (n) 10
Sunday 3
supermarket (n) 5
sure (adj) 8
surname (n) 1
sweater (n) 9
swim (v) 6
swimming pool (n) 4

T

T-shirt (n) 9
tablecloth (n) 14
tail (n) 11
take (v) 5
talk (n) 11 (v) 9
tall (adj) 11

taste (v) 8
taxi (n) 2
tea (n) 8
teach (v) 18
teacher (n) 1
team (n) 16
technology (n) 13
telephone (n) 1
telephone call (n) 4
television (n) 3
tell (v) 5
temperature (n) 10
tennis (n) 6
test (n) 7
theatre (n) 4
then 3
there (adv) 2
thing (n) 2
think (v) 6
thirsty (adj) 7
thrilling (adj) 10
through (prep) 7
ticket (office) (n) 4
tie (n) 14
tiger (n) 11
time (n) 3
tired (adj) 7
title (n) 11
to (prep) 4
toast (n) 8
today (adv) 7
together (adv) 12
toilet (n) 2
tomato (n) 7
tomorrow 4
tonight 4
too 3
tourist (n) 16
town (n) 5
tracksuit (n) 7
train (n) 2
training (n) 12
transport (n) 2
travel (v) 17
trousers (n) 9
truck (n) 6
try (v) 18
turn (v) 2,5
turning (n) 5

U

uncle (n) 1
under (prep) 2,7
underground (n) 2
Union Jack (n) 12
university (n) 6
unlucky (adj) 14
use (v) 4
useful (adj) 11
useless (adj) 11
usually (adv) 7

V

vacuum cleaner (n) 5
vegetable (v) 7

vegetarian (adj) 8
vertical (adj) 12
very 4
video (n) 9
vinegar (n) 8
visit (v, n) 10
visitor (n) 1
vocabulary (n) 1

W

wait (v) 18
waiter (n) 8
walk (v) 6
walnut (n) 8
want (v) 4
war (n) 16
warm (adj) 10
wash (v) 7
wash up (v) 15
washing (n) 15
watch (n) 2 (v) 3
water (v) 15 (n) 7
way (n) 5
wear (v) 7
weather (n) 10
wedding (n) 14
Wednesday 3
week (n) 10
weekend (n) 6
well (adv) 12
west (adj) 10
wet (adj) 6
whale (n) 10
what (n) 2
when 3
where 2
which 4
white (adj) 8
who 6
whose 11
wife (n) 1
wild (adj) 10
wine (n) 8
winner (n) 7
with (prep) 1
wonderful! (adj) 12
wood (n) 14
woodwork (n) 13
wool (n) 9
word (n) 1
work (n) 3 (v) 3
world (n) 10
worried (adj) 18
worry (v) 6
write (v) 1
wrong (adj) 10

Y

year (n) 10
yellow (adj) 9
yoghurt (n) 7
young (adj) 9

Z

zoo (n) 10